Working Memory

Improving Your Memory for the Workplace

Alternatives
Life Options for Today

Working Memory
Improving Your Memory for the Workplace

BILLY ROBERTS

LONDON
HOUSE

First published in Great Britain in 1999 by
LONDON HOUSE
114 New Cavendish Street
London W1M 7FD

A catalogue record for this book is available
from the British Library

ISBN 1 902809 06 8

Edited and designed by DAG Publications Ltd, London.
Printed and bound by Biddles Limited,
Guildford, Surrey.

Contents

Introduction

How often have you said, 'I can't quite remember – it's on the tip of my tongue' or perhaps 'The face is familiar, but the name escapes me'? Everyone experiences these annoying lapses of memory, and knows only too well just how frustrating and sometimes extremely embarrassing they can be. I am quite sure too, that most people have missed an important appointment because it had not been entered in the diary and simply 'slipped the mind'.

We nearly always make excuses for our absent mindedness, blaming age or a poor memory. But the truth is there is no such thing as a poor memory. We may have difficulty in recalling a piece of information from the memory bank of our mind, but our inability to locate the correct compartment does not in any way constitute a poor memory.

Unless your job involves a great deal of mental interaction, you probably do not fully understand your memory and the way it works. We nearly always take our memory for granted. If something cannot be recalled when needed, it is all too easily accepted as the way it has to be.

Most people have their own methods of recalling a memory to mind. How often have you found yourself in the awkward situation of being greeted by someone whose name you could not remember, and have found yourself mentally flicking through the alphabet until his or her name suddenly sprang into your mind? I am certain that the majority have experienced this and been saved from the embarrassment of saying, 'The face is familiar, but I am afraid the name escapes me'.

Some memories are stronger and much clearer than others, particularly when they are associated with joyful or sad events. It would seem that when the consciousness has been impressed by an event, the memory of it is strong and easily recalled. The mind is a

vast mental library in which our memories are catalogued and categorised in two sections, 'Important' and 'Unimportant'. Important
memories are those that have made an impression and are therefore
easily recalled.

If you are to remember something, it has to be made interesting to enable it to make an impact upon the mind. This is most
certainly the case when studying for exams, or perhaps learning
lines for a speech or play. If your interest is not stimulated, the
memory of it is feeble and nebulous and therefore unlikely to be
recalled.

However, even a boring subject can be made interesting with a
little imagination and visualisation. Creative recall makes swotting
for exams less of a chore and far more fun. Learning to place information in that category of the memory marked 'Important' is easier
than you might think. Instead of your memory letting you down
when you most need it, with the correct technique and minimum
effort, you can make it work for you.

Even those who are fortunate enough to possess retentive
memories are limited with what exactly they can do. The retention is
usually short-term, often just long enough to help them get through
exams, or for whatever reason the information is needed, then it is
often forgotten.

Our memory is sometimes extremely selective. However, it can be
encouraged to broaden its interest and what it chooses to recollect.

Most people convince themselves that their memory is poor and
are forever saying, 'I can't remember anything. I have an awful
memory!' This attitude is negative and self-destructive, and merely
chastises the memory rather like one would scold a disobedient child.
By adopting this attitude, the mind is being conditioned into believing
it is ineffective, making it even harder for memories to be recalled.

Instead of constantly decrying your memory, it should be spoken
to in a gentle, positive way and offered encouragement as one would
to a pupil who is not doing very well at school. The memory certainly
responds positively to this sort of treatment, but must also be
trained in the same way as a child.

When I first began to explore the concept of memory training, I
realised early on just how easily one might be discouraged from

using some methods. I found many of the techniques available to be so complicated and technical that a good memory was needed before even considering using them! Some of the simplest systems are quite often the most effective. It was with this in mind that I decided to compile a less complicated programme, one that would appeal to almost anyone.

How many times has a certain fragrance in the air caused a childhood memory suddenly to come into your mind? Perhaps a Spring sky has brought happy memories flooding back. This phenomenon of association is quite common and forms the basis of an extremely effective method of memory recall that I shall detail later. It may well be that you choose to create your own method of remembering, or perhaps find it easier to work with the integration of more than one system. Do so if it works for you.

Although many mnemonists dismiss the suggestion that the memory can be developed with exercise in the same way as the muscles of the physical body, also included is a programme I have designed specifically for that very reason. However, in order to improve memory recall, your powers of concentration and ability to focus must first be cultivated. Aided by extremely effective visualisation techniques, it *is* possible to improve your memory by at least sixty per cent – or even more!

We have only a superficial encounter with the people and circumstances we come into contact with during the course of the day, and pay very little attention to what we see. Little wonder we have difficulty in remembering details. However, even events taking place in the periphery of our vision are registered by the brain and stored in the subconscious. Nothing is ever lost.

A prime example is when someone is placed under a hypnotic trance to help them remember an incident in which they were not directly involved. When the mind has been made quiet, it is possible to encourage memories to surface from the subconscious to the conscious. I think this proves that nothing is forgotten, but simply pushed into a different compartment of the mind, where it stays until needed.

There have been so many books written on the subject of memory you would be forgiven for not knowing which offer the best techniques. The truth is they are all very similar and offer more or less the same methods so employ techniques that work for you. At the end of this book you may feel you can create your own methods. Use them if they are effective.

1
The Cupboard System

As a child, I used to write details to remember in a special little book, which I checked each day. This system appears to work for a lot of people and most certainly did for me. However, occasionally I would climb into bed exhausted at the end of a very busy day to find things coming into my mind that I needed to do the next day and which I had not put down in my book. Too tired to do anything about it, more often than not I fell asleep, nearly always forgetting the following day what it was I had to remember. I am sure many have experienced this more than once in their lives and know only too well how frustrating it can be.

Obviously, when only eight or nine I was completely unaware that there are techniques to help you to remember, but like most children at that age I used to create my own. Without even realising it, I began adopting a method of remembering that has been used for centuries and which I found effective.

This involved mentally creating a cupboard, into which I placed whatever I needed to remember. Although the technique appears to be simple, preparatory work is necessary to make it work properly. There would be little use in simply visualising a cupboard and placing in it the points to remember. The exercise has to be set up and programmed before it will work efficiently.

To do this you need to call upon your powers of visualisation and the ability to focus your concentration without allowing your mind to wander. The images you create should appear very clear and solid on the screen of your mind and not be weak and nebulous. Try to make them three-dimensional so they appear as real as possible. Only when you can produce such images will the exercise really work for you without any effort whatsoever. Once you have created the imagery and established the programme, putting items to remember in the cupboard will be as real as hanging clothes in a wardrobe.

Before even thinking of using your cupboard and activating its power, you need to sit quietly for a few moments in a comfortable chair.

Close your eyes. Breathe slowly and deeply, relaxing your body as much as you can. Pause for a few moments between each inhalation and exhalation, making your breathing evenly spaced.

Watch the empty screen of your mind and slowly create a cupboard just in front of you. So that your cupboard can easily be recalled, give it an unusual or endearing feature. Make it brightly coloured, perhaps cartoon-like in appearance. Bestow it with any feature that will help you to re-create it with ease. It must have the same appearance every time you use it.

Determine all you can about your cupboard, noting every minute detail. Repeat the same process once a day for at least a week – longer if necessary – before you begin to use it. When you are absolutely certain that the mental imagery has been established and programmed, try the first experiment, perhaps in bed.

To make sure that the cupboard technique is going to work properly for you, for the initial experiment you should mentally deposit a few items of no importance, objects picked randomly out of the air. A knitting needle, a cup and perhaps a light bulb could be carefully placed in the cupboard. Ensure that the objects are not connected in any way.

When you are nice and relaxed in bed and feeling comfortable, close your eyes. Picture the cupboard looking very bright and clear in your mind. Open the door mentally and look inside. Now randomly select three objects and carefully put them inside your cupboard. Make a mental note of exactly where you placed each item. Focus on them individually for a few moments and close the door.

Before allowing the imagery to fade, place a number three on the front of the cupboard, just to remind you how many objects you have deposited inside.

Focus your attention on the cupboard for a few moments longer, then breathe slowly. As you exhale, allow the picture in your mind gently to fade away.

Remember that the objects you have mentally placed in the cupboard for the initial experiment must be chosen randomly and have no special significance or importance. There is no need to fall asleep whilst thinking about the contents. If the exercise was correctly performed, in the morning all the contents should be revealed to you. Upon rising, mentally create your cupboard and open the door to see the objects you need to remember.

Once you are certain the experiment has worked, extend the time of recovery. For example, place your items in the cupboard one night and retrieve them two days later. This ensures that the randomly chosen objects are not still fresh in your mind, but have genuinely been retrieved mentally from the cupboard.

The next step has to be followed very carefully so do not rush it. Remember to look upon the cupboard as your personal memory filing system that must be checked every day.

To allow the cupboard method to remain programmed so it will operate every time, it should be regularly revitalised, whether or not you are using it to remember details. Ensure that you mentally recreate it every day. This will only take a few minutes of your time, but to make it work well, it should be visualised regularly.

By now, you should have an extremely good memory filing system that will spring into action no matter how much you need to remember.

You do not have to be in bed to use this system, for it will operate anywhere at any time. It may be that you need desperately to remember a list of items in a shop window, or perhaps the names of people you have just met, but are unable to write down at that moment. Simply deposit whatever you need to recall in your mentally created cupboard to be retrieved whenever you need it. Get into the habit of checking your memory filing system every day, just as you would your letter-box each morning.

With repeated use, the cupboard system becomes stronger and increasingly efficient. Although best to visualise the cupboard as being the same in appearance every time, it might change of its own accord. Allow this to happen. Once the technique has been fully established, the subconscious mind sometimes begins to be actively involved, thus producing more effective memory expression. You may find that in twelve months it does not remotely resemble the method with which you first started: this is all right.

You might wonder how on earth you can mentally recreate a memory cupboard whilst standing in the middle of the High Street.

Once you have mastered the technique, it will not be necessary for your eyes to be closed. You will find it quite easy mentally to recreate your filing system anywhere. Images may be created with your eyes open as you become proficient at visualising.

When rapport has been built between you and the method, the cupboard will gradually be by-passed, so to speak, and eventually dispensed with completely. Although the cupboard system is highly effective when the memory is poor, it is really only a tool with which to fashion a much sharper and subtler memory. In other words, the cupboard is merely a prop until the technique has been mastered and the 'key' located.

The longer you work with and use the cupboard as a means of accessing your subconscious, the greater your mental range when recovering memories.

Taking the method a little further and increasing your memory's capacity, you can substitute the items you put in your cupboard for letters and numbers. For example, if you need to remember to buy a pen, some soap, a ball of string and a packet of paper-clips, simply deposit the first letter of each article into the cupboard – 'P', 'S', 'S' and 'P'. Mentally close the door. As you did before, put a number – this time it is four – on the door to remind you how many articles you placed inside.

The main reasons for not being able to recall memories are lack of attention, poor concentration and an inability to observe. In the 'Introduction', I wrote it is my belief there is no such thing as a poor memory. Most people who claim to suffer from them usually have lazy or butterfly minds.

There is a great difference between an ineffective memory and one that is simply not used properly. Paying careful attention is the first step in the cultivation of a good memory. Taking notice of details and developing your powers of observation are a prerequisite in the development of good memory recall. The cultivation of a good memory does not just mean paying attention only visually. It involves all the senses – sight, touch, taste, smell and hearing. Not to use all of them is to limit the information you are able to retain.

Learning to focus your attention is easily done with a little practise. Once you have mastered the technique, your mind becomes a mental radar-scanning device, able to recreate at a moment's notice any information it has recorded.

Instant recall can be cultivated with the development of visualisation. Learning to visualise encourages the mind's powers of observation and precipitates the creative faculty. More people than you think dismiss the idea of being able to visualise, as though it were an ability possessed by certain kinds of special individuals and not everyone. In fact, we all have the ability potentially to visualise and create images in the mind. Even those who find it difficult can most certainly be taught the technique.

Looking at something and recreating an impression of what you have seen in the mind's eye is an integral part of memory recall. It is quite easy to train the mind to develop this ability, though the accuracy of detail recalled is solely dependent upon how much attention you have paid.

It is exactly the same when meeting people for the first time. Our ability to remember their names is also dependent upon how much notice we take when we encounter them initially. Even though we are politely introduced, we normally pay very little attention, so the next time we meet their name escapes us completely. Most people go through the procedure of introductions mechanically, often not even looking at the person to whom they are being introduced. Little wonder that many individuals find it difficult to remember the names of those they have only met superficially.

Unless something makes an impression, it is highly unlikely that we will be able to remember it with any detail. To strengthen the memory means improving your powers of observation. How to remember people's names and faces will be covered later on, so now we will try a little experiment.

To test your powers of observation, take a pencil and note pad. Write down all the items you can remember that are in your bedroom. Try to be as detailed as possible. Make a note of how the furniture is positioned. What is on the window ledge? How many objects are on the dressing table? What is beside the bed? Take time in mentally picturing the bedroom.

Although you may think you are familiar with your bedroom, you will be surprised at just how little notice you have taken of it. When you are making a note of everything you can remember, it is important to try and pay particular attention to detail. The positioning of furniture is not as vital as personal little items, such as trinkets, ornaments and clothes. The idea is for you mentally to recreate the room as best you can, noting every minute detail. This experiment will help you to perceive just how little attention you pay to detail. We mostly see only the obvious. When training the memory you must notice everything, whether it is important to you or not.

You may like to take this experiment further. Take a walk down the local High Street. Later, get a friend to ask you questions about the shops. Try to list them in order, stating what they sell. Describe the street in detail. You may have walked down it a thousand times or more, but will be surprised just how difficult it is to recall it in any great detail.

Write down everything you can remember in the High Street. When you have finished, return to see how accurate you were. Indeed, you should put your powers of observation to the test as much as you possibly can. Pay great attention to detail. Exert your powers of observation and concentrate. Attention, observation and concentration collectively constitute the key to a good and effective memory.

You can also aid the memory processes with rhythmic breathing. Breathing slowly and deeply helps you to control your thoughts. By focusing the breath in a precise, deliberate manner it is possible to recall those deeper memories. Breathing in this way is also very useful when creating your mental cupboard. Exhalations should be used to vivify the mental imagery whilst inhalations help to create the bond between yourself and the cupboard, thus allowing your mind to exert greater control over the exercise.

When creating your mental cupboard remember to make it very brightly coloured – almost surrealistic or cartoon-like – as this will impress the mind's imagery faculty. Know every last aspect of the cupboard so it is clearly defined in your mind.

Some people 'build' two different cupboards, each used to store different memories. You might like to try this approach. It may seem a little too complicated, but when you have established the mental images in your mind and charged them with specific thoughts, you will have no trouble at all using them. This method works of its own accord, requiring very little effort on your part.

The mental exercise of this particular system helps to train the mind to focus, thus preparing it for the following methods of memory recall. It is extremely important to keep the mind as active as possible when endeavouring to cultivate and strengthen the memory. Visualisation and concentration should be integral parts of your daily programme, for when combined these will help the natural memory immensely.

2

The Figure Alphabet System

The main and most probably the only causes for an inability to remember are poor concentration, lack of attention and insufficient observation. Although there are many methods to improve the memory, this system is perhaps the most effective and, I think, more useful than any other available technique.

Once the following system has been fully mastered and you have found the key to it, you will very quickly appreciate its practical value. Although it is often considered one of the most complex of memory systems, when you have grasped its underlying fundamental principles, the whole concept of remembering dates and figures will be transformed completely. Forgetting birthdays, telephone numbers and important appointments will become a thing of the past.

Often called the *Major System*, the Figure Alphabet System was devised by Stanislaus Mink Von Wennsshein in the mid-seventeenth century. His intention was to produce a system that would enable the user to convert letters into numbers and vice versa with the incredible possibility of creating innumerable combinations of words, letters and figures.

Professor Loisette, one of the earlier pioneers of memory training, refers to numbers as 'abstractions', and most difficult to remember. Therefore, to make them easier to recall we must simply convert them into words. This is because words make mental pictures and so can more easily impress the mind. Once the words are recalled, they can then be converted back into the numbers from which they were originally created.

In this method, figures are converted into words, but vowels (A. E. I. O. U.) have no numerical value. Neither do the letters Y and W. This system is an excellent method for remembering dates and telephone numbers, but must be perfectly committed to memory.

However, as long as the general rules are observed very carefully you should have no trouble at all using the technique.

The nought and the nine figures are represented by the following consonants:

O by *S, Z*, or *C soft*
1 by *T, D* or *TH*
2 by *N*
3 by *M*
4 by *R*
5 by *L*
6 by *J, SH, CH* or *G soft*
7 by *K, C hard, G hard, Q* and *NG*
8 by *F* and *V*
9 by *B* or *P*

Before making any attempt to convert numbers into words, you should learn the numerical value of the consonants. But do not forget that vowels have no numerical value and are only used to make up words.

For example, the word *SEE* = O. The letter *S* has the value of O. The double vowels of *E* have no numerical value at all. The word *SAY* = O. Nought represents the letter *S* whilst the vowel *A* and the consonant *Y* have no numerical value. Other examples of words represented by *O* are *SOW* = O. *EASE* = O. *IS* = O.

Two consonants with the same value appearing in a word together with no vowel between them are counted as one consonant with the value of one letter. For example, *'LL'* = 5, *'NN'* = 2, *'RR'* = 4, *'DD'* = 1, and so on.

In the word 'accident', the first two consonants have different numerical values. The first 'c' has the value of 7, the second the value of nought. 'Accident' then = 70121.

As silent consonants have no numerical value, they are therefore disregarded. For example, the 'b' in Lamb = 53. Comb = 73. Tomb = 13.

Here are other examples where the letters are silent and therefore have no numerical value: The 'gh' in 'Bought' = 91. The 'gh' in 'Neighbours' = 2940. The 'k' in 'Know' = 2. The 'l' in 'Could' = 71, or the 'p' and 'l' in 'Psalm' = 03.

The equivalents of the figure-consonants have the same value of the consonants themselves. For example, 'gh' in 'Tough' = 18; 'gh' in 'Enough' = 28; 'gh' in 'Rough' = 48; 'ph' in 'Phrase' = 840; 'ph' in 'Nymph' = 238; 'ck' in 'Lock' = 57.

Sometimes the sound of a word can be quite deceptive so one needs to listen very carefully. 'Ng' is not always represented as 7. When they sound separately, they should be treated as such, as in the word 'Engage' = 276.

'Ci' and 'Ti' – and sometimes 'Si' and 'Sci' – represent 'Sh', as in 'Gracious' = 7460. 'Nation' = 262. 'Conscience' = 72620.

The 'dge' in 'Judge' stands for 'J', so the word 'Judge' = 66.

'Tch' stands for 'Ch', which = 6, as in 'Pitch', which = 96. 'Ch' sometimes = K, as in 'Christmas', which = 74030.

In words like 'Pleasure', the 's' stands for 'sh', which = 6. 'Pleasure' therefore = 9564.

Remember only to use vowels with which to make words. They have no numerical value and are discarded, as are the letters W and Y. Words such as 'Weigh' or 'Whey' contain no numerical value and are never used.

In cases where one word ends with a consonant and the following word begins with the same consonant, each letter is calculated separately and both are given separate numerical values. For example, 'That Tide' = 1111.

This technique is also sometimes referred to as the Phonetic System, and is probably the most sophisticated and certainly the most adaptable of all mnemonic methods. But once mastered, its possibilities and advantages become endless, thus enabling the user instantly to retrieve phone numbers, dates, anniversaries, etc.

The endless combinations of consonants and vowels make the coding of figures into words simple once the system has been fully grasped. This can then lead to discovering other methods of coding and retrieval.

Always remember that in this system it is the sounds of the consonants that are the most important, not the consonants themselves. To help you appreciate this, look at the following list so you can familiarise yourself with the similarity of the sounds of the various groups of words. Pay particular attention to the way the mouth is held in the formation and pronunciation:

Number 1 – Though, Toe, Doe
Number 6 – Jaw, Shaw, Chow, Gem
Number 7 – Key, Quo, Cow, Go
Number 8 – Foe, Vow, Fee
Number 9 – Pay, Bay
Cipher O – Zero, Zoo, See, Cell

Becoming accustomed to the various sounds of the words is important in this system as it will help you greatly when formulating a
method of working. The number 6 has only three sounds because J
is the same as soft G. The number 7 has two sounds, hard C and Q,
which are the same as K. The cipher O has two sounds, soft C is the
same as S.

Attention is drawn to the sound of the words because the
various letters and their combinations can sometimes take on the
same sounds. This is seen in the 'sh' sound that is also produced by
the S in the word 'Sugar'. It is likewise apparent with the C in
'Ocean', the 'ci' in 'Gracious' and with the 'ti' in 'Ratio'.

The structure or the way a word looks can often be deceptive, as
seen with the words 'Ratio' and 'Patio', where the letter T sounds
differently. Other examples are apparent in 'Ace' and 'Act'. As you can
see, the consonant C is sounded differently, one being hard, the
other soft. In 'Ago' and 'Age', the letter G is also sounded differently.
The 'Gh' in 'Ghost' – and also in 'Tough' – take on a completely
different sound, as do the 'Ch' in the words 'Church' and 'Chronic'.
The hard and soft sounds of 'ng' are also noticeable in 'Singe' and
'Sing'. So is the S in the word 'Sore' as opposed to 'Sure'. 'Sore' = 04,
but 'Sure' = 64.

Care should be taken when listening to the letter X as in some
cases this takes on the consonant sounds of K and S. Although it is
nearly always pronounced as 'Ax', it is also occasionally sounded as Z
as in 'Xylophone'.

Similarly, care is necessary when using certain words, such as
'Accent'. The two consonants of C have different numerical values:
the first C has the value of 7 whilst the second C = O. The word
'Accent' = 7021.

A repeated consonant can make the same sound and so is
treated as having the same numerical value. Words like 'Cotton' =

712, not 7112, as the double 'tt' is counted as one sound. When two consonants together make the same sound, they are also counted as having one numerical value, as the word 'Pack' = 97, not 977. Another example, 'Ascent', equals 021, not 0721.

In your analysis of this system it is important to consider the sounds of the words just as much as what you can see. Remember that silent consonants have no numerical value as in 'Knife' = 28, and not 728. Another is 'Could' = 71, not 751. In this case, the 'l' is silent so therefore has no numerical value.

Uncertainty can sometimes arise when encountering certain words, such as 'Measure' or 'Vision'. The sound 'zh' is mostly treated as 'sh' so is given the numerical value of 6.

As mentioned earlier, another letter and sound combination that occasionally presents a problem is the 'ng' sound, as in 'Sing' and 'Sang'. This can be counted as hard G, and has a numerical value of 7. However, sometimes the 'ng' is counted as two distinct letters, N and G, with different numerical values. I would reiterate that you should allow the sound to influence you. You will need practise before being able to translate the letters on sight into the correct code. Just like reading music, once you have found the key and fully mastered the technique, converting letters into numbers and vice versa will become second nature.

This system is an ideal way for remembering details where figures of any kind are involved. Addresses, birthdays, phone numbers, ages, dates and financial data are just a few things which can be recalled with this method. It is an effective mental filing system complete in itself. Once mastered, very little effort whatsoever is needed to use it. The most effective and useful way in which this method can be employed is to convert numbers into meaningful words or phrases. Those that catch the imagination can easily be remembered, and then converted back into the numbers from which they were originally created.

Perhaps I need to remember a doctor's appointment at 1 pm on December 17. To make it easier, I think of another more humorous term for doctor. 'Quack' is catchy and easier to recall. Quack is the noise made by a duck. An example of a phrase I can use to help me to remember my doctor's appointment is 'The Duck Tune'. 1, 17, 12 – 1 pm, 17th of 12th. Of course, this is just one of many examples. If you use this system regularly, you will soon be able to devise your own codes.

Perhaps I also have to remember the registration of a friend's car. This is C767 MDM. Immediately, the MDM appears to me as 'MaDMan'. Converting the 767 into the code, I can create the phrase 'CATCHING A MaDMan'.

I cannot stress enough just how important it is that you develop the ability to listen to the sound of the word. With practise, your ears become more sensitive and attuned. You may find the sounds of some words quite difficult to distinguish, but this will be overcome with patience and determination.

In the process of converting words to figures, it should always be borne in mind that the word must be treated as it is sounded and not as it is spelt. 'Tomb' has a numerical value of 13, and not 139. 'Pleasure' sounds very like 'Plezhur', so has a value of 9564, not 9504. 'Passion' is pronounced 'Pashon', with a numerical value of 962, not 902. Similarly, 'Thought' sounds like 'Thaut'. Therefore, its numerical value is 11. Remember that X sometimes sounds like KS. For example, 'Box' has a numerical value of 970. 'Trough' sounds like 'Trof', and has a numerical value of 148. Words such as Eye, Owe, You and Weigh have no figure value.

Before we proceed further, study the numerical value of the consonants already given. Try to fix these firmly in your mind, then move to the following exercise to see what you have learned. Find the figure value of the following words:

a)	TRUTH	n)	RADIATE
b)	LIAR	o)	CRESCENDO
c)	POOR	p)	MONUMENT
d)	RICH	q)	LACQUER
e)	GOVERNMENT	r)	PHEASANT
f)	ESTABLISHMENT	s)	COMMON
g)	KNOCKING	t)	XYLOPHONE
h)	INCOME	u)	XENOPHOBIA
i)	MASSIVE	v)	GENTLEMAN
j)	ORNAMENT	w)	COTTAGE
k)	EMPIRE	x)	CHALET
l)	CHAMBER	y)	BALLET
m)	RIDDLE	z)	ZOOM

If you had no trouble finding the numerical value for these words, you can safely assume that you understand the basis of the Figure Alphabet System. Now check your answers:

(a) 141. (b) 54. (c) 94. (d) 46. (e) 78232. (The 'r' has been omitted because it is not sounded.) (f) 1956321. (g) 277. (h) 273. (i) 308. (j) 42321. (k) 394. (l) 6394. (m) 415. (n) 411. (o) 74621. (p) 32321. (q) 574. (r) 8021. (s) 732. (t) 582. (u) 289. (v) 621532. (w) 716. (x) 65. (y) 95. (z) 3.

By this stage, you should have got them all correct. If not, study the numerical value of the words a little more. Be diligent with both their sound and the visual aspects. It is important not to skip over the figure values, thinking that you know them off by heart. Learn them properly so you appreciate all the numerical values and are able to recite them at random. Only then will you be ready to adopt the system in the way that it should be used.

Once you fully understand the basis of the Figure Alphabet System, you will see that there are various ways in which it can be employed. One can either use all the sounded consonants in the conversion of figures into words or phrases, or just the initial consonants, depending on the length of the phrase. This is also a matter of preference and how quickly you are able to convert the figures into the appropriate words. Professor Loisette gives the following examples:

The Great Wall of China is 1,250 miles long. This piece of information may be remembered by converting the figures into the phrase, '_Th_ey _n_ow a high wa_ll_ _s_ee' (1250). Translating this phrase will give back the figure value and the answer to the question, 'How long is the Great Wall of China?' Answer: 1,250 miles long.

This following example will also help you to see how the system can be used.

Egypt's greatest pyramid is 479 feet high. Professor Loisette suggests the phrase (4) 'World's (7) Greatest (9) Pyramid' to help remember this fact.

The world of pop was devastated when John Lennon was brutally murdered in New York City on December 8, 1980. This more recent piece of history may be recalled with the phrase (8) 'Fall (1) down (2) never (1) die (9) Beatle (8) fourth (o) sing'. 8. 12. 1980.

You must remember never to use the same word to represent two different dates. For example, its first two consonants for one date, and its two middle and the first and last consonants to represent another.

Always be diligent in your choice of words and the way in which you connect them to the facts of the events. Take care in your analysis when associating the word or phrase with the information you need to recollect.

New York was founded by the Dutch in 1626, and was then known as New Amsterdam. To remember this historical fact, Professor Loisette suggests using the phrase (1) 'Dutchman (6) chose (2) New Amsterdam (6) Joyfully'. You should always consider your choice of phrases very carefully, taking time to connect them with the date.

Figures by themselves are always difficult to remember. This is possibly why some people have a head for maths and others do not.

Committing a long series of figures to memory in the usual conventional way is not completely impossible, but for the majority of people the process of learning them by rote presents something of an arduous task. However, when a line is broken up into groups, memorising them becomes much easier, especially when the numerals are converted into appropriate words. First of all, try memorising these numbers by reading them a few times, and see how you do:

31415729535653993238462947353 27

Unless your memory is exceptional, I would imagine that you did not get very far. As explained, figures are abstractions, and therefore difficult to memorise. But when converted into meaningful words, they become much easier to visualise and consequently to memorise.

314	157	295	356	539
Mother	*Delicate*	*Noble*	*Malicious*	*Lamp*

323	846	294	735	327
Monument	Fresh	Neighbour	Commotion	Maniac

Fix the words in your mind. They will give you back the numbers in any order you like, forwards or backwards. You may be able to improve the technique and adapt it in some way to suit you. Remember to learn the numerical value of all the consonants before you attempt to use the Figure Alphabet System.

As previously stated, all the sounded consonants of a word can be used, but sometimes only the initial consonants of each word in the phrase are employed. Take every opportunity to practise converting words into numbers and numbers into words. Advertising bill boards will immediately present a sequence of figures whilst car number plates give you letters and words almost straight away. Use the Figure Alphabet code system in everything you do until you are totally familiar with it and the way it works. Once mastered, this method will prove to be an ideal memory aid.

A great deal of time should be spent studying the sounds of the words and their numerical value. Although this may seem to be somewhat arduous, you can rest assured that with the potential and many uses of the Figure Alphabet technique your efforts will be rewarded.

Adopting this system, numerical information can be coded into words and phrases specifically designed to be used as a sort of mental filing system. The possibilities are endless once the method is fully understood. Unlike other numerical techniques, the Figure Alphabet System is not limited to the number of key or peg-words that can be used. Indeed, two-digit numbers can be converted into one word using the initial consonant sound to represent the first figure, and the last consonant sound for the second figure. Here are some examples for code words for the figures one to twenty:

1 = lie	6 = jaw
2 = know	7 = key
3 = may	8 = view
4 = ray	9 = pie
5 = low	10 = toes

11 = dad		16 = dish	
12 = tin		17 = tack	
13 = tomb		18 = tough	
14 = tire		19 = tip	
15 = deal		20 = nose	

You can, of course, design your own words by working out the numerical value. You should do so as much as possible to help you fully grasp the concept of coding figures into words.

Selecting key words that are meaningful to you can be fun and serve as incredible memory aids, helping you to remember almost anything. Because the Figure Alphabet System makes use of the sounds of words, it is sometimes known as the Phonetic System. It is amongst the most versatile of all techniques, and one that is known psychologically to improve the memory.

At this point, it might be a good idea to put what you have learned to the test. First of all, using 'D' to represent the number 1 in all cases, create words from 10 to 19 using the Figure Alphabet System.

By now, you should have no trouble with this exercise. If you encounter any difficulties, refer to the following list of one hundred key words that will help you.

Figure Alphabet System Exercise

Figure	Letters	Word
10		
11		
12		
13		
14		
15		
16		
17		
18		
19		

Think carefully about the words you use: they should be mean-ingful to you. Once you have mastered the art of converting the figures into words, you should begin to see just how sophisticated this system really is.

Hundred Key Words for the Figure Alphabet System

1 Lie	26 Nash	51 Light	76 Cage
2 Know	27 Neck	52 Lane	77 Cake
3 May	28 Navy	53 Lamb	78 Cough
4 Ray	29 Nip	54 Liar	79 Cap
5 Low	30 Moose	55 Lull	80 Face
6 Jaw	31 Mat	56 Lash	81 Fat
7 Key	32 Man	57 Lake	82 Fan
8 View	33 Mime	58 Laugh	83 Foam
9 Pie	34 Mire	59 Lap	84 Four
10 Toes	35 Mile	60 Chase	85 Full
11 Tot	36 Mash	61 Chat	86 Fish
12 Tan	37 Muck	62 Chain	87 Fog
13 Dome	38 Mafia	63 Chime	88 Five
14 Door	39 Map	64 Chair	89 Fob
15 Dull	40 Race	65 Cello	90 Base
16 Dish	41 Rat	66 Cha-cha	91 Bat
17 Duck	42 Rain	67 Chuck	92 Bin
18 Dive	43 Ram	68 Chaff	93 Boom
19 Dip	44 Roar	69 Chip	94 Bar
20 Nose	45 Roll	70 Case	95 Ball
21 Nod	46 Rash	71 Cat	96 Bush
22 Noon	47 Rock	72 Can	97 Black
23 Name	48 Rough	73 Cameo	98 Beef
24 Near	49 Rabbi	74 Car	99 Babe
25 Nail	50 Lace	75 Call	100 Daisies

When creating the key words, try to be as imaginative as possible. To give you a far wider range of word ideas, you might find it helpful to use a dictionary. Once your list of words has been created, familiarise yourself with each one. Remember to be as consistent as you can with your choice of words. Here are a few more examples of how you can use the Figure Alphabet system.

You may have to remember that the Empire State Building is 1,250 feet tall. One memory training writer suggests that you imagine the building filled with tunnels (1,250). As you can see, the word 'Tunnel' is the key word.

The same writer also suggests that to remember the height of the highest waterfall in the world – it is in Venezuela and falls 3,212 feet – we might recollect that it is as high as a mountain (3,212). Here, 'Mountain' is the key word.

It makes it easier to recall if the key word or phrase has a meaningful connection to whatever it represents, but this is not essential. Even disconnected words are still far easier to remember than abstract numbers. However, it is much more fun when the key word has a connection to whatever you need to remember.

Professor Loisette gave some very interesting examples in his treatment of the subject of memory recall, in which he also highlighted the mistakes some students of the subject make. He stressed the importance of making absolutely certain that the correct numerical value was used when converting numbers into letters. The simple error of converting the number 2 into M or 3 into N can completely throw the code word out of context, thus giving an incorrect answer. This is why it is so important to be diligent in your study of the numerical value of all the consonants and their sounds. Here are some further examples:

Tea was first introduced into Europe in 1601. To recall this piece of historical information, we can use the code words Tea Chest. These words are meaningfully connected, and give the user the numbers 1601.

It may not always be possible to create such meaningful words or phrases, but as long as they are unusual or humorous, you should have no difficulty recalling them.

The longest river is the Nile at 4,090 miles long, flowing into the Mediterranean Sea. To recollect this information, you could use the code Rain Ceaseless Prince Sun. This coded sequence gives the length of the river – 4,090.

The highest mountain in the world is Mount Everest in the Himalayas, which is 29,145 feet high. To remember this fact, you could employ the coded phrase 'Never pace the rough lane'. Although not directly connected to Mount Everest or its height, it is most certainly easy to recall and immediately gives back the figures 29,145.

These are just a few examples of how the Figure Alphabet System can be put to use. Experimentation is most important to enable you to formulate your own method of working with the number word method.

Remember to learn the numerical value of the sounded consonants until you have fully mastered the technique.

Coding Chart

O	1	2	3	4	5	6	7	8	9
S	t	n	m	r	l	sh	g hard	f	b
Z	th						j	k	v	p
C soft	d					ch	c hard		
						g soft	q		
							ng		

Use this chart as a point of reference. Try to fix it firmly in your mind. With a little practise you will be able to dispense with writing down the figure code and to recall it mentally without any great effort.

3

The Figure Word Sound System

Although the Figure Alphabet System is thought to be the most complex and certainly more difficult than any other memory system to learn – unless you have a natural ear for sound – the following may prove equally as arduous to take in mentally. However, once the fundamental principles and rules have been learnt and fully mastered, you will find it an invaluable aid to memory improvement.

It is important to be diligent when learning the rules. Only when you totally understand them and can tell at a glance the numerical value of the sound of the word will you be ready to put the system to use.

Reference is made in the following rules to ten numerals representing ten different categories of sound. Repeat aloud the word examples along with the sound of each corresponding number. For instance, ton – one, son – one, can – one, fan – one, etc. This must be practised until you fully understand the connection between the sound of the number and the sound of the corresponding word.

Syllables ending with p,b, l, d and th cannot be used, except when long vowels are involved with their sound. In these cases, you will be unable to translate the word into a number.

Some examples of sounds that cannot be used because they bear no resemblance to the sounds of any numbers are top, tib, til, ted and teth. But by combining them with long vowels, there is a similarity so they can be adopted. For example, type, tribe, tile and tied all represent the number 5. Tube, tool and tooth denote the number 2.

But remember this: only when you associate the five sounds that cannot be used with long vowels are you able to convert them into numbers.

The primary element suggesting each number is the approximating sound of each syllable. Therefore, one syllable stands for one number only, two syllables for two numbers, three syllables for three numbers. For instance, de = 3; delude = 32; delusion = 321.

The Figure Sound System embodies a fundamental concept that purely and simply makes use of numbers to represent similar sounds found in the syllables that make up the words in our language. Five of the rules are based solely upon the vowel sounds: U = 2; E = 3; I = 5; A = 8; O = O. The remaining five depend entirely upon the consonants, and the consonant sounds with which the syllables end.

Any syllable which contains a blunt-sounding M or N when following the strong vowels A, O and U represents the number 1. Examples of this can be seen in the word sounds TON, SON, CAN, FAN, HUM, DRUM, GUN, RUN, etc.

Syllables producing the vowel sounds of a long U or OO – or any similar sound – denote the number 2. Example word sounds are TIME, FUME, PLUME, LOOK, BOOK, NOOK, SHOE, PEW, VIEW, KNEW, DREW, YOU, etc.

Other syllables causing the vowel sound of long E represent the number 3. Instances are found in the word sounds of TREE, ME, SEE, BE, FLEA, FLEE, FREE, KNEE, KEY, GLEE and PLEA, or when it is sounded long before D, as in ENDED, MENDED, etc.

Syllables producing R as the primary sound stand for the number 4, as in the word sounds FUR, FOR, FAR, OR, ERR and CAR, and in the sound of COMMANDER.

Syllables producing the vowel sound of a long I or the dipthongal sounds of OI or OY represent the number 5, such as in the word sounds BOY, BUOY, TOY, SOIL, OIL, KITE, LIGHT, NIGHT, RIGHT, TIME, LIME, RHYME, CHIME, etc.

Any syllable sounding X or K as the primary or concluding sound represents the number 6. For instance, there are the word sounds of MIX, FIX, BOX, FOX, BRICK, SICK, DOCK, LOCK, ROCK, etc. This also applies when a syllable is concluded with a hard sounding G or C – BIG, TWIG, FIG, DIG, etc.

Syllables with the sounds of S, V or F as the primary or concluding sound represent the number 7. Try these word sounds – DISH, FISH, LASH, CASH, DEAF, MUFF, LIVE, DOVE, LOVE, etc.

Any syllable producing the vowel sounds of a long A represents the number 8 as in RAY, MAY, SAY NAY, LAY and BAY. This is also applicable to any syllable concluding with T, in which T is the primary sound – BAT, SAT, POT, HOT, KIT, HIT, etc.

A syllable containing a sharp-sounding M or N when following the weak vowels E and I represents the number 9. Think about the word sounds of LIMB, RIM, PIN, PEN, HEN, etc. However, this only applies when the vowel in the syllable does not exhibit its long sound, and M or N is the primary and concluding sound, as with these examples.

Syllables producing the vowel sound of a long O represent the cipher O. Try these: DOE, MOW, SOW, LOW, MOLE, SOLE, SOUL, COAL, HOLE, ROLL, POLE, LONE, HOME, MOAN, etc.

You should now be able to see that this particular system involves the sounds of the words and not the spelling. It may take a while to master this method, but once you do so, rest assured that it will prove to be an extremely versatile and useful aid to improving your memory.

You must accustom yourself to the different sounds of words. For example, GRATITUDE produces a short sound, with the letter 'I' giving it the numerical value of 3. However, when the 'I' is associated with 'N' and produces a full sound, as in the words PINE, LINE or even NINE, it may have the numerical value of 9, in fact exactly as it sounds. When 'O' is sounded in association with 'R' – as in SORE, CORE, MORE or FOUR – it might have a numerical value of 4. So does the wider sound of 'A' as in PA or MA. DA may also produce a numerical value of 4. The word sounds of RUSSIA and PRUSSIA amount to a numerical value of 74 as does USHER.

It should also be borne in mind that when a syllable is concluded with two sounding consonants, only the numerical value of the first one is considered in the analysis, as in the word sounds MONK, MONG, AND and ANT, which all have a numerical value of 1. Other examples are the word sounds CART, MART, BURN, TURN, HARD and BARD, with the numerical value of 4. The concluding sound of *ING* always has a numerical value of 9.

We are usually only able to remember information that has pleased or impressed us. Details that we need to recollect are often those which are difficult to recall. Memory aids support the memory and help it to focus. In the long term, this stimulates and thus improves one's ability to remember even the most insignificant data.

Fully understand how this system works before any attempt is made to use it. Try to develop your ear for the different sounds of words, practising as much as possible.

Do so with the following list, making a note of your analysis of the numerical value of each word. Answers may be checked at the end of the glossary that concludes this chapter.

POSTMAN	MANHOLE
MONKEY	TRUMPET
MOONLIGHT	MOONLIT
PEACOCK	CHARCOAL
ARSON	POISON
LIFEBUOY	BLACK HOLE
DOG FIGHT	KNICK-KNACK
BUCKET	CROSSROAD
ASTUTE	SAPPHIRE
MYSTIC	MISTAKE
PUSHING	MOTTO
SATIRE	MATTRESS

Try not to be too disappointed if you had difficulty with some of the words as practise will ensure more positive results. Should you not have an ear for the different sounds, it may take you some time to tell a word's numerical value at a glance.

You may want to check your results before you take a look at the following glossary.

Glossary of the Numerical Value of Word Sounds

Example Word Sounds Representing Nought
SHOW, SLOW, SNOW, SOW, SO, THROW, THOUGH, TOE, TOW, BOW, BLOW, CROW, DOUGH, DOE, FLOW, FOE, GLOW, GO, HO, HOE, LOW, LO, GROW, KNOW, MOW, NO, OH, ROW, SEW, WOE, LOAD, MODE, ODE, ROAD, RODE, STRODE, TOAD, DOZE, FROZE, CLOSE, HOSE, CHOSE, NOSE, ROSE, PROSE, POSE, THOSE, COLD,

FOLD, BOLD, GOLD, HOLD, MOULD, OLD, SCOLD, SOLD, TOLD, COAL, BOWL, DOLE, GOAL, POLE, SCROLL, ROLE, MOLE, SOUL, STOLE, TOLL, WHOLE, COACH, POACH, BROACH, HOME, COMB, DOME, FOAM, ROME, GLOBE, ROBE, JOB, PROBE, BOAST, GHOST, ROAST, HOST, COAST, MOST, POST, TOAST, BLOWN, SOWN, FLOWN, GROWN, LONE, LOAN, MOAN, PRONE, STONE, THRONE, TONE, CONE, OWN, HOPE, COPE, POPE, ROPE, SOAP, SCOPE, DOPE, BOAT, COAT, FLOAT, GOAT, GLOAT, VOTE, WROTE, NOTE, DOTE, ROTE, STOAT, BLOAT.

Example Word Sounds Representing Number One
FUN, RUN, GUN, NUN, DONE, SUN, STUN, BOND, POND, FOND, TONE, TON, SON, WON, RAM, DAM, HAM, STRONG, THONG, CHAMP, TRAMP, CRAMP, DAMP, LAMP, CAMP, STAMP, FONT, WANT, PUMP, RUMP, PLUMP, DANCE, LANCE, GLANCE, TRANCE, CHANCE, BAND, GLAND, GRAND, DRUM, GUM, DUMB, HAND, LAND, STRAND, STAND, CAN, FAN, RAN, MAN, TAN, SCAN, ANT, CHANT, GRANT, PLANT, SLANT, AUNT, BUNG, RUNG, BANG, CLANG, RANG, SLANG, SWAN, CON, ON, ONE, NONE, BUNT, PUNT.

Example Word Sounds Representing Number Two
GOOSE, LOOSE, MOOSE, USE, HEW, HUE, JEW, KNEW, SHOE, SCREW, BLEW, BREW, CHEW, CREW, DO, FEW, FLEW, GLUE, GREW, YEW, YOU, FOOD, BROOD, MOOD, ROOF, PROOF, BOOK, COOK, BROOK, SHOOK, MULE, YULE, SCHOOL, FOOL, COOL, STOOL, POOL, BLOOM, ROOM, TOMB, SPOON, JUNE, PRUNE, MOON, SWOON, SOON, SOUP, HOOP, SCOOP, STOOP, TROUPE, LOOT, BOOT, ROUTE, SHOOT, CHOOSE, LOOSE, NEWS, USE, NOOSE, GOOSE.

Example Word Sounds Representing Number Three
SEA, BEE, FLEE, FREE, STEEL, STEAL, WHEEL, DEAL, ZEAL, DREAM, CREAM, TEAM, KEY, PLEA, ME, PEA, WE, TREE, GREASE, FLEECE, NIECE, PEACE, CEASE, BEAST, PRIEST, FEAST, EAST, BEACH, BLEACH, EACH, BREECH, PEACH, SPEECH, EAT, CHEAT, FEET, FEAT, GREET, NEAT, HEAT, TEACH, BEAK, BLEAK, CHEEK, FREAK, BREED, BLEED, FEED, GREED, LEAD, FREED, SEED, READ, WEED, GREEK, MEEK, WEAK, PEEK, CLEAR, DEAR, DEER, FEAR, YEAR, HEAR, WEEK, SNEAK, DEAL, HEEL, KEEL, KNEEL, PEEL, PEAL, REAL, CLEAVE,

GRIEVE, EVE, LEAVE, SLEEVE, THIEVE, WEAVE, BREEZE, FREEZE, BEAM, REAM, SEEM, SEAM, QUEEN, SCREEN, BREATHE, SHEATH, WREATH, SHEET, STREET, SLEET, SWEET, REED, NEAR, REAR, SMEAR, KEEP, LEAP, WEEP, REAP, PEEP, SHEEP, SLEEP, EASE, PLEASE, SQUEEZE, SNEEZE, WHEEZE.

Example Word Sounds Representing Number Four
HEART, PART, START, SMART, TART, CART, BIRCH, CHURCH, LURCH, SEARCH, SWORN, CORN, THORN, BORNE, CURVE, SWERVE, NERVE, BIRTH, EARTH, CHURL, CURL, FURL, GIRL, EARL, PEARL, ARE, JAR, BAR, FAR, STAR, WAR, CURSE, HEARSE, NURSE, VERSE, AIR, BARE, PAIR, CARE, DARE, FAIR, HARE, STARE, SWEAR, THEIR, LEARN, CHURN, FERN, WHERE, WEIR, THIRD, WORD, CORD, LORD, WARD, CURB, HERB, VERB, BURKE, LURK, BURST, CURST, PURGE, VERGE, SERGE, THIRST, WORST, CURSED.

Example Word Sounds Representing Number Five
HIVE, DIVE, THRIVE, ICE, VOICE, SLY, TRY, STY, SPY, BY, BUY, CRY, DIE, FLY, EYE, BRIDE, CHIDE, DIED, DYED, GLIDE, GUIDE, HIDE, PIKE, SPIKE, STRIKE, WIFE, KNIFE, STRIFE, TIME, SLIME, WIPE, GRIPE, PIPE, RIPE, SNIPE, TYPE, SIRE, SQUIRE, SPIRE, TIRE, SITE, SPITE, SIGHT, MITE, MIGHT, PRIDE, SLIDE, TIDE, WIDE, HIDE, BRIGHT, BITE, FIGHT, KNIGHT, TIGHT, PRIZE, GUISE, WISE, SIZE, SCRIBE, BRIBE, TRIBE, JIBE.

Example Word Sounds Representing Number Six
EGG, DREG, KEG, LEG, PEG, ACT, PACT, TRACT, TACT, SICK, THICK, WICK, FIX, MIX, STICKS, BOX, FOX, COX, CLOCK, COCK, SOCK, CHICK, BRICK, KICK, LICK, FROCK, FLOCK, KNOCK, LOCK, MOCK, ROCK, SHOCK, PICK, NICK, QUICK, PACK, QUACK, RACK, SLACK, BACK, BLACK, JACK, CRACK, SEX, NEXT, TEXT, STOCK, DUCK, LUCK, PLUCK, STUCK, WRECK, CHECK, TUCK, TRUCK, BIG, DIG, PIG, FIG, WIG, SPRIG, FLECK, PECK, SPECK.

Example Word Sounds Representing Number Seven
CLIFF, STIFF, SNIFF, GIVE, LIVE, DOVE, LOVE, GLOVE, PEST, TEST, REST, NEST, WEST, LUST, BUST, THRUST, CRUSH, BRUSH, BUSH, FLUSH, RUSH, GUSH, FUSS, THUS, TRUSS, BLESS, CHESS, DRESS,

LESS, MESS, PRESS, BEST, LEST, BREAST, DUST, CRUST, MUST, JUST, ASH, CASH, CRASH, LASH, BRASS, ASS, CLASS, GAS, GLASS, RASH, DASH, MASH, THRASH, MUFF, ROUGH, TOUGH, CUFF, LAUGH, STAFF, THEFT, LEFT, DRAUGHT.

Example Word Sounds Representing Number Eight
PLATE, GATE, HATE, MATE, LATE, AID, GLADE, STRAIN, PAIN, GAIN, TRAIN, VEIN, CHAIN, CAIN, CAT, CHAT, MAT, RAT, HAT, BRACE, MACE, CHASE, STAKE, RAKE, MAKE, SNAKE, TAKE, HASTE, TASTE, WASTE, APE, CAPE, BIT, GRIT, HIT, SIT, KNIT, RAIN, REIGN, AIM, BLAME, CAME, FLAME, BET, DEBT, JET, GET, LET, SWEAT, THREAT, DOUBT, SPOUT, SHOUT, TROUT, BATHE, LATHE, SCATHE, SHADE, RAID, TRADE, QUAIL, RAIL, TALE, VEIL, WHALE, FEIGN, LAIN, PLAIN, PLANE.

Example Word Sounds Representing the Number Nine
VINE, WINE, WHINE, KIND, FIND, MIND, BLIND, NINE, LINE, MINE, PINE, THEN, WHEN, WREN, SHINE, SIGN, SPINE, SHRINE, SWINE, FRIEND, LEND, MEND, GRIN, INN, KIN, PIN, SIN, TIN, SKIN, SPIN, THIN, WIN, TWIN, DIM, GRIM, HEM, STEM, THEM, WENT, VENT, HYMN, HIM, LIMB, SKIM, SLIM, RINSE, BEN, DEN, GLEN, KEN, HEN, PENCE, HENCE, DENSE, WHENCE, SENSE, SWIM, TRIM, TIM, HIM, KIM, MEN, PEN.

Numerical Value of the Words Previously Given

POSTMAN = 18	MANHOLE = 10
MONKEY = 13	TRUMPET = 18
MOONLIGHT = 25	MOONLIT = 28
PEACOCK = 36	CHARCOAL = 40
ARSON = 41	POISON = 51
LIFEBUOY = 55	BLACK HOLE = 60
DOG FIGHT = 65	KNICK-KNACK = 66
BUCKET = 68	CROSSROAD = 70
ASTUTE = 72	SAPPHIRE = 75
MYSTIC = 76	MISTAKE = 78
PUSHING = 79	MOTTO = 80
SATIRE = 85	MATTRESS = 87

Remember that the words in the glossary are merely to give you an idea of how the system works. Once you have grasped the basics, you will be able to search for your own. The main point is to develop an ear for the sounds, then the fundamental principles become apparent, and the whole concept much easier to understand.

As you become accustomed to using the sounds of words, you will increasingly employ all your senses. Numerical and word information that has been stored in the memory banks can be accessed and recalled with speed. However, like all memory systems practise does make perfect – and practise is vitally important.

Most people find that they can modify a memory system to suit their own requirements and mental abilities. But unless the correct mental application is introduced nothing whatsoever will be achieved. It would be foolish to dismiss a system of memory improvement on the basis that it appears far-fetched or too difficult to use. Lack of concentration is probably the key factor in the inability to cultivate a good memory. When combined, observation and concentration are the primary factors of an efficient and good memory.

Remember, too, that it is just as important to listen to the sound of a word as it is to see it written down. Try to train your ear by listening to conversations around you, mentally making a selection of words to convert. To help sharpen your sense of hearing, it is a good idea to listen to the radio or watch television with your eyes closed. By doing so, you will become accustomed to the different sounds of words, making converting them into figures a lot easier.

4
Studying for Exams

The prerequisites of a good memory are impression, retention and recollection. Should any of these be impaired, the memory suffers as a direct consequence. Before moving any further, let us take a look at these three mental factors.

Impression fits into two categories – those produced by the imagination and through the mind's own mental processes, and others entering from outside sources. However, even impressions created by the imagination sometimes originate from external sources.

Retention is primarily determined by the degree of interest in the first impression and how exactly it holds the concentration.

The strength and vividness of the first impression – plus the degree of emotion to which it is attached and the associations it creates – collectively determine the ease of recollection.

Although certain impressions originate in the mind, others enter from outside, reaching the brain through the senses. Thus, upon meeting a person for the first time, his or her appearance makes an impact upon the brain. The strength of this is solely dependent upon two aspects – interest and observation. Without interest, the impression is weak – and more than likely difficult to recall – so it needs to be made interesting to impress the mind.

A student may encounter difficulty studying for exams if the subject matter does not stimulate his or her interest. Learning by rote can be arduous and ineffective as information acquired in this way is often only retained until the exams are over. To fix what has been learned firmly in the mind requires a little more effort and a completely different approach other than repetition.

For example, when learning the positioning of musical notes on the stave, mnemonic techniques are employed. The phrase 'Every Good Boy Does Fine' helps the student fix the line notes E, G, B, D,

F firmly in the mind. The word FACE is used to represent the notes in the four spaces. The same technique can be adopted to enable you quickly to learn the different musical keys with their sharps or flats. In the Major scale, the Key signature of G is one sharp, D two sharps, A three sharps, E four sharps and B five sharps. These can easily be recalled with the phrase 'Great Dishes Are Easily Broken'.

The keys with flats are F with one flat, B with two flats, E with three flats, A with four flats and D with five flats. These may be remembered with the phrase *Flat Bead,* the letters in italics giving the correct order of the flats.

Similarly, the colours of the spectrum are much easier to remember when converted into the word VIBGYOR. This is composed of the first letters of Violet, Indigo, Blue, Green, Yellow, Orange and Red.

The days in each month of the year are recalled with greater ease when the following is recited: 'Thirty days hath September, April, June and November. All the rest have 31, excepting February alone which has 28 days clear, and 29 each leap year.'

We rely upon mnemonic aids nearly every day. At the beginning of the book, I gave the example of flicking mentally through the alphabet to remember someone's name. It is important when using methods to employ one that works for you, regardless of whether or not it is a traditionally accepted memory aid.

I read about a young woman who was a Licentiate of the King and Queen's College of Physicians of Ireland. Using the letters L, K, Q, C, P, I, she came up with, 'Licensed to Kill, Qualified to Cure, Patients Invited'. This is a humorous and meaningful way of using the initial letters of what one needs to remember, and obviously an effective method of lodging such a complicated title in the mind.

When it comes to more extensive information, the process of learning and fixing the subject matter in the mind to be recalled when needed becomes more difficult. Even when one has an aptitude for learning by rote, the natural memory cannot always be relied upon to give back the information when it is required. Therefore, a little help and encouragement are often needed. Let us take the Welsh word LLANFAIRPWLL, GWYNGYLLGERTRO, BWLLGERCHWYRN, BYLLGOGERBWLL, LLANTYSILIO, GOGOGOCH.

Unless you have an understanding of the Welsh language, this is most hard to pronounce, let alone learn. Any attempt to memorise such a difficult line simply by repeating it – no matter how many times you do this – would also probably prove to be impossible. However, when we follow the next procedure, at least half the Welsh word could be learned in a few minutes. Simply break the word down into syllables. Analyse each one, sounding it out aloud as you do so:

LLAN FAIR PWLL, GWYN GYLL GERTRO, BWLL GERCH WYRN, BYLL GOGER BWLL, LLAN TYSILIO, GO GO GOCH.

Also analyse the first three syllables, and sound the individual letters out aloud. Similarly, slowly sound the first and second syllables a few times before adding the third syllable. Recite all three syllables one to three, then in reverse. Notice that the following three syllables all begin with G. Pay particular attention to the way in which these three syllables are structured and how different they are from each other. Sound the middle syllable, then the one on the left, next the one on the right. Now sound them all. Begin with the first syllable, concluding with the sixth one.

Notice the relationship between the second letter in the third and fourth syllables. This association will connect the first group of three syllables to the second group of three syllables.

Note how the syllable BWLL is like PWLL. One will remind you of the other. The first half of the word is concluded with GERCH.

You should find the second half of the word a lot easier to learn. To begin with, you should not attempt to fix the whole word in your mind. Initially, concentrate on the first half.

When approaching the remainder, deal with it in much the same way. Analyse the first syllable of the second part of the word, sounding the individual letters out aloud. Again, notice the similarity between the second and fourth syllables. Familiarise yourself with these as one will help you to recall the other. See a connection between the third, seventh, eighth and ninth syllable. Combined, all four will form an association, each causing the other to come to mind. Once you feel quite comfortable with the second half, attempt to bring all the syllables together by reciting each one from LLAN to GOCH.

This method of learning may appear somewhat simplistic, but it is a technique that always works. The ability to spell even the most difficult words is often developed with the use of this system. Always break difficult sounding words or words that are hard to spell into syllables. The same technique may be applied when endeavouring to learn long lists of numbers, as shown in an earlier chapter. Provided the list or passage is broken down into groups and each group is addressed individually, almost anything may be learned.

Of course, the Welsh word is only an example. This technique can be used for long passages, such as pieces of prose or speeches. Although it can be adopted for much longer projects, unless your natural memory is good, it would be advisable to apply this method only to fairly short tasks.

Regardless of the content and length of the subject to be learned, concentrated attention is vitally important if you are to secure a perfect impression in the mind. A poor memory is mostly the result of a butterfly mind or one with an inability to concentrate and observe. This is down to pure laziness or lack of effort. An effective memory needs to be worked at and encouraged. It is not produced without mental application.

Studying for exams can be hard and soul destroying, especially when the subject matter does not stimulate the interest. Fixing information in the mind is difficult at the best of times, but when forced to study a topic which is of no interest at all, it becomes almost a punishment. But it *is* possible to make studying fascinating and enjoyable: the information *can* be embedded in the memory to be recalled at any time.

When faced with the arduous task of learning long passages or a subject that fails to stimulate the imagination, the following suggestions will make the procedure livelier.

Carefully read through the text two or three times, making no attempt to learn the contents or to memorise any part. Focus the attention upon the main points. Try to secure a clear impression of these in the mind. On a separate writing pad, make a note of the passages that appear to stand out and which somehow impress you. Slowly scan the material once again, strategically selecting one strong word in each paragraph to be used as a memory point. Make a mental note of these, familiarising yourself with the area of the text in which they are to be found.

Slowly read through the text, pausing momentarily at each memory point. At the same time, mentally scan the text for the passages that impress you. Read through two pages at a time, backwards and forwards, always being conscious of the memory points.

When you have repeated this process several times, close your eyes and try to recreate the text in your mind, using the memory points to help you. See how much text you can recite with your eyes closed, all the time keeping the memory points firmly fixed in your mind. With regular practise, the more each point will mentally bring forth the rest of the line, and then the whole paragraph.

The passages of which you have made a note will help to create a link from one memory point to another, and should also help you to grasp the substance of what you are studying as opposed to simply memorising the words without any understanding of what you have learned.

Although it may take some time mentally to absorb the full content of the text, this method is more effective than learning by rote. The use of memory points is important to fix the information permanently in the mind. Although I have suggested using one strong word in each paragraph, you can employ words at any strategic point. Once accustomed to using memory points correctly, you may find yourself creating them in a pattern throughout the entire text.

You can also apply 'Phantom memory points' to help mentally assimilate the substance of what you have learned. These are words that bear no relation whatsoever to the text, and have merely been interjected at strategic points simply to 'remind you' of the text and to help secure it in the memory. Although bearing no relation to the content of the text, a Phantom memory point appears to have an association with what is being studied by fitting into it and yet being out of context. This can be humorous, depending upon how you use the word and its position. Take a look at the following example of how a Phantom memory point may be used:

As Elizabeth slowly ascended the stairs, she could feel Rebecca's eyes following her *toes*. When she had reached the top of the stairs, Elizabeth turned to look down at Rebecca. Before she had a chance to speak, Rebecca said, 'Tummy! Elizabeth I am so sorry.' Elizabeth smiled before turning to continue to her bedroom.

You can create Phantom memory points anywhere. As explained, they do not have to be in context with the rest of the text, or even make a great deal of sense, as long as they help you mentally to recall the content and get the substance of what you are studying.

Phantom memory points are not suitable for everyone. Although the method may appear a little silly, it can be very effective as a method of 'linking' the memory when endeavouring to remember what has been learned. The conventional memory point technique will work for anyone, provided the following advice is fully and carefully observed.

All surrounding activity or noise must be eliminated completely from the area as distractions of any kind are the main cause of forgetfulness. Concentration is a primary factor when involved in serious study, so I would suggest that periods of learning should not exceed one or two hours at a stretch. Longer than this would cause you to lose concentration and defeat the whole object of the exercise. If you want to grasp the substance of the text and not just simply commit the words to memory, your concentration must be totally consistent to ensure that the content of the work may be recalled at any time.

It is entirely a matter of choice how you select the memory points in the text. They are simply used as points of recognition to help you to remember. In themselves, the memory points possess no magical formulae for remembering, but are merely aids to assist in the sometimes difficult process of recalling information to the mind.

Here is an example of how memory points may be used to learn an extract of prose entitled 'The Hunt'. Once you understand the concept of the memory point system, see how long it takes you to commit this piece of prose to memory. Again, the words in italics are the memory points.

The Hunt
The early morning mist rises with shame to reveal the *flash* of crimson coats. No idle chatter from the hunters' lips can

conceal the deathly smiles, nor *magic* away the guilt that is yet to come, but even now is felt.

Excited hounds, hungry yet fed, filled with eagerness for the chase, mingle with *impatient* horses, whose frozen breath disappears with the rising mist, but still the guilt of the hunters' deathly smiles remains.

Already the blood of the hunted flows, but only in the minds of the hunters, as they rub the cold from their *frosty* hands and don their caps with pride.

The misty sky reveals a curious *sun*, who peeps slyly, then retreats with shame, as the signal is given and the hunt begins, but for the hunted it is already over.

A wide-eyed creature stares from the safety of the hedge, but its safety is soon to be broken by the crimson coats, and *howling* dogs, *sounding* horns and horses at a gallop, but led by the hunters' deathly smiles.

Confusion! And with hesitation the gentle creature surrenders.

Alas! No prisoners taken in this gruesome war, as a *curious* sun *peeps* once again, and the crimson coats congratulate each other with outstretched hands. But the hunters' deathly smiles slowly disappear, and the crimson coats turn to coats of bloody *shame* . . . The journey home is always dark, but only in the minds of the hunters.

The examples are merely to give an exact idea of how memory points can be used to aid your studies. When endeavouring to cement a larger text in the mind, it is a good idea to employ the use of several or more memory points per chapter. Once you have selected the words and points, it is sometimes more helpful, particularly where serious and academic subjects are concerned, to write the memory points down on a separate piece of paper, linking them together so that they form some sort of association.

For example, writing 'The *FLASH* of the *MAGIC* sword *EXCITED* the crowd and made the king *IMPATIENT*' may bring Flash, Magic, Excited and Impatient together. Doing so in this sort of association helps to lodge the memory points in the mind. These are just suggestions. You may have your own ideas of how to link memory points.

As stressed, a good memory is quite often needed to begin with before some memory aids can be used at all. They often appear quite complex and difficult to learn. However, there are no substitutes for a natural memory, though some of the simpler mnemonic methods often help train and give rise to a more efficient memory.

But as with any other mental ability, the memory can be developed and cultivated with the use of exercise. Most people are lazy thinkers, putting very little effort into their thinking processes. Ordinary thinking is quite simple and takes place of its own accord. However, the process of remembering is different and calls for some effort. It has to be met halfway. In order for the mind to remember, it needs to be focused, especially when studying for exams or endeavouring to learn a speech.

As figures are usually hard to remember, for this very reason they are extremely effective in training the   concentration   and   the memory, as one does not function without the other. Try the next exercise to see how well you can recall figures.

Recite the following numbers several times out aloud, focusing on each one in turn as you do so. Allow them to make an impression upon the mind, almost as though you were taking a mental photograph to look at later on:

3, 7, 9, 2, 5, 1, 6, 4, 8.

Having recited the figures, when you feel confident that the mental impression is strong enough to enable you to recall them, close your eyes and allow the numbers to be reproduced on the blank screen of the mind. Still with your eyes closed, recite the figures mentally once or twice in the correct order. Then do so in reverse. Next, repeat them in the correct sequence several times, concluding with the reverse order.

Notice how much concentration was required to deliver the figures in reverse order, and exactly how long it took you.

If you found this mental exercise easy, you should increase the amount of figures by five and repeat the process. Remember that figures are abstractions, and therefore sometimes difficult to recall. Fixing them in the mind in this way helps to cultivate the memory and make it stronger.

For the next exercise we will follow the same procedure, but use letters instead.

Take a look at the following line of capitals, spending only a couple of seconds on each one in turn. Do not allow your concentration to become a labour as this will defeat the object. After you have focused upon each letter, let your eyes scan the whole line backwards and forwards a few times:

X, I, L, P, V, B, Z, O, Q, W, M, G, S, U, Y, A, C, J, D, K.

Give yourself no more than three minutes to memorise all the letters. To cement them firmly in the mind, the following procedure should be followed.

Read the letters through very slowly, making a mental note of each one. Repeat the process at least five times, before doing the same in reverse order.

When you have concluded the suggested process, close your eyes. Instead of trying to see the whole line of letters in your mind, focus the attention mentally on the 'X', making this the memory point. At this stage, do not permit any other letter to come into your mind. Now mentally move your vision to the following letter, 'I', and see no other apart from this. Spend only a few seconds on the 'I'.

Still with your eyes closed, mentally move to the letter 'L', and do the same here. Follow the same procedure with all the letters until you are quite certain you have memorised them. When you are fairly confident you can recall them without any great effort, mentally flick through all the letters one last time.

When this has been done successfully, follow the same procedure in reverse order, mentally reciting all the letters. This will probably prove to be a little more difficult. However, with practise you will become proficient in the art of visualisation and recall. This technique will aid you in the development of eidetic vision, helping the development of your natural memory.

Should you encounter difficulty in memorising all the letters, I would suggest breaking them up into groups. This makes it easier to memorise long lists of figures or letters. The same principles can be applied when learning lengthy text. Trying to lodge too much at once in the mind defeats the object. If you are too ambitious, you will most certainly forget that which you are aspiring to remember. Of one fact you can rest assured – you must learn to have total faith in your memory. Neither underestimate it nor treat it as being inferior.

Depending on the theme and content, some text is quite easy to memorise, even for those with an average memory. Lyrical poetry, for instance, is far easier to learn than prose because the rhyme and rhythm allow one word to suggest another, thus often implanting it permanently in the mind. More effort and concentration are needed with prose or any text possessing no obvious theme. When endeavouring to fix the substance of a lengthy text in the mind, the student should be quite relaxed, both mentally and physically. The mind must be totally focused on the text. Then read in stages.

Time and care should be taken when reading the text and substance, and the main theme studied very carefully. At this point, try not to worry too much about learning the content. Concentrate more on getting the gist of the subject matter.

In a similar way to the memory points, you should highlight the first word of each paragraph. Familiarise yourself with these words, using them as memory keys. With practise, you will find that the memory key word will suggest the word following it, thus triggering the whole line, and so on.

De-stressing the Mind

Setting exercises for your memory and putting it to the test are the ideal ways of developing and training it. Mental exercises may be used to precipitate the memory processes and also to aid the student when studying for exams. Apart from this, two aspects must not be overlooked, although they are often taken lightly. These are the physiological and psychological effects of stress often experienced when studying.

Stress causes shallow breathing, tension and headaches. Combined, such symptoms cause an inability to concentrate. Very little can be achieved when these conditions are experienced, and yet they can be so easily overcome. Here is how.

Find a comfortable chair. Relax for a few moments, with your eyes closed. Before you begin the process of relaxation, ascertain your normal heartbeat by placing your fingers on your pulse and count mentally from one to six. Each heartbeat is measured as a 'pulse unit'. The units of inhalation and exhalation should be the same. The units of retention and between breaths should be one half the number of inhalation and exhalation. In this exercise, you should breathe in to the count of six pulse units, hold it for the count of three, breathe out to the count of six, hold it for three, and so on.

Once this rhythm has been established in your mind, place your hands gently on your lap and commence breathing rhythmically. Remember to make the inhalations and exhalations slow and evenly spaced. Each time you exhale, allow yourself to relax deeper and deeper.

As you inhale a complete breath, feel its force clearing all tension and anxiety from your body and mind. Experience your mind becoming quiet and serene, and the body totally relaxed.

Allow your mind to drift from the counting and be conscious only of the inhalations and exhalations, feeling the breath passing through your brain, making your mind quiet, yet very clear.

As you breathe in, mentally say 'Relaxed', and as you breathe out, 'Calm'. Use these two words as personal mantras to relax you whenever you feel stressed. The relaxation period should last for at least ten minutes before studying. Always conclude the relaxation with a few moments of quietness.

Practised regularly, you should feel rapid benefits. Once you have accustomed yourself to this method of relaxation, tension and anxiety can be dispelled very quickly. If at any time of the day or night you feel stressed or anxious, you have simply to close your eyes for a few moments and silently intonate the words 'Relaxed' and 'Calm' – relaxed as you breathe in, calm as you breathe out.

Rhythmic breathing helps to control the release of adrenalin – the primary cause of anxiety and stress – and aids concentration and your powers of recall. In the long term, your capacity mentally to retain information will increase greatly, a development that should have much wider implications and affect the sensitivity of all the faculties. Controlling stress through the process of rhythmic breathing also helps to improve the confidence and general health, and will allow you to study for much longer periods without losing concentration.

The following mathematical mental teaser swept the country some years ago. Try to work it out in your mind without writing it down. The answer is nearly always the same and will be given at the end of the book.

Think of a number between one and ten. Multiply it by nine. Add the digits so that you get a single number. Take away five. Now, taking A as one, B as two, C as three, etc., work out the letter that corresponds to your new number. Think of a country beginning with that letter. Now select an animal beginning with the second letter of your country. What colour is the animal?

5
How to Remember Faces

When being introduced to someone for the first time, we very rarely pay attention to the details of the meeting, such as the name of the person or facial appearance. Although quite important, these points often go straight over our heads. We often smile out of politeness, but mostly the moments of introduction are usually experienced with our eyes either to the ground or even staring through the person as though they were made of glass.

In the business world such introductions are often somewhat mechanical, unless the individual to whom we are being introduced is a potentially important contact. If so, we tend to make an effort purely for selfish reasons.

It can be extremely embarrassing not to remember the person's name on a second meeting. But all it takes to recall faces and names is a little practise at paying attention and being more observant. Respect and admiration are nearly always given to those who immediately remember one's name after just one previous meeting. It says a lot about someone who has obviously shown an interest and made an effort.

What to Do Upon Being Introduced
a) Upon shaking hands, look the person in the eyes and see the face.
b) Take in hair colour, shape of face, and most of all colour of the eyes.
c) Notice the way in which the individual concerned is attired. Is he or she smartly dressed?
d) Pay attention to fragrance and overall presentation.
e) Make a mental note of any distinguishing aspects, such as a large nose, bushy eyebrows or ears that stick out. These sort of noticeable features may help you to remember the person's name next time you meet.

f) When a name is given, listen and make a mental note of it.
g) Should the name be unusual, ask for it to be repeated and, if necessary, spelt.
h) Pay attention to what is said during the meeting.
i) Allow as much eye contact as possible during the conversation, but without making the other party feel uncomfortable.

What Not to Do
a) When introduced, do not look at the ground.
b) Do not permit your mind to wander even for a moment when the person is talking.

Unless an individual is important to you in some way, it is unlikely that their name will leave an impression upon your mind. Most people are only able to remember the names of those with whom they have had some sort of association, whether in a business or social situation. Indeed, very few people make an effort to remember names. Faces are different: we can often recognise most with some ease.

We generally have no problem at all remembering the names of famous people whose faces are constantly seen in magazines or on television. The visual impression constantly reminds us of their names. Nor do we usually have any difficulty recalling the names of those with whom we are in regular contact. It is the names of those with whom we have only a superficial encounter that mostly cannot be remembered. Because they are not that important, their names are only sounds and have not made any impression. In fact, anything we find difficult to remember has held very little interest for us when the first impression was made. In order to make a lasting impact, the subject must be interesting to us.

Faces are no exception. I am not suggesting that you should find everyone fascinating. This is not possible. But it *is* feasible to show an interest in all those with whom you come into contact.

Make a detailed analysis of their face: the shape, the colour, the eyes, nose and ears. When you hear the person's name, try and associate it with some physical characteristic. For example, Mrs Sharp might have sharp, pointed features which will help you to recall the name. On the other hand, Mrs Swan has a long neck that reminds you of her name. Then there is Mr White, who always appears pale, just as his name implies. As you can see, someone's name might suggest something about their appearance, making it easier for you to recall.

Additionally, an individual may have a distinguishing feature, such as a birthmark or scar, that will help you to recollect their name. If your job involves interacting with different kinds of people and is dependent upon your communicative skills, the onus is on you to be observant and remember the names of all those with whom you come into contact work-wise. Lack of interest in people you meet reflects badly upon your professional and business status. A little effort really and truly goes a long way.

Every time you think of a person, always recall their name at the same time, regardless of whether or not you are interested in them. Try to keep the mind as active as possible when training it to remember names. Upon the first introduction, always use someone's full name, if you know it. If you do not, ask for it, even if it is not absolutely necessary. Allow the name to create a visual image in your mind. Mentally say it a few times to secure it in your mind.

Try to avoid saying 'Mr What's-his-name?' Always make the effort to learn the name of the person to whom you are speaking. Disciplining yourself in this way and being extra observant aids the cultivation of a sharp memory with excellent recall. Even on the telephone, listen carefully to the sound of the voice at the other end. If it is someone you have never met, try to form a mental image of how you think they look. Gain a picture of their colouring, the shape of their face and even their height. You may think this a pointless exercise, but if you really want to improve your ability to remember names and faces, it should be an integral part of your training programme.

When looking for unusual facial characteristics, the whole face and its individual parts must be considered in the analysis. The shape of the nose might suggest the person's name. Perhaps it is a Roman nose, or Greek. Then again, it may be an aquiline nose or very straight, a broad nose or even narrow, and very pointed. Remember that the shape of the nose can be the main feature on a face and may help you to recollect the person's name.

The mouth, too, plays a major part in the face's overall appearance and is often the first point to attract our stare when we meet someone for the first time. Thin lips can give a person a fairly hard appearance, or make them look quite serious, miserable even. Full lips may sometimes show someone to be happy or fun loving, causing the face to be transformed with a simple smile.

Bushy eyebrows might make the face mysterious or even humorous. Narrow bow-shaped brows could give an almost cartoon-like appearance if someone has big eyes and a large, elongated nose.

Narrow cat-like eyes often cause a feline appearance when accompanied by long lashes. The overall shape of the face, the cheekbones and the way it is framed by the hair can give an almost spontaneous appearance. Meanwhile, a bald head and a round face indicates a strong appearance, or represents a happy, jolly individual. The thin, elongated face with eyes that are close together may have a sly appearance. All of these characteristics can help in recalling someone's name.

Ears must also be considered in the overall analysis of a person's face. Close to the head, they tend to give a specific appearance, perhaps quite serious or possibly hard. Ears that stick out can make the face look comical, especially if an individual has an unusually shaped nose.

These are just suggestions of what you ought to consider when analysing a person. Try to use anything that catches your attention to help you recall a name. The personality should also be considered in your assessment. In short, call upon any observation to assist you.

To fix an individual's name solidly in the mind, it is a good idea to repeat it a few times out aloud whilst looking at them. The reason for this is to produce a mental connection between the visual appearance and the sound of their name. This will strengthen their image in the mind so that a strong impression is made in your memory to be recalled when you next need it.

Any peculiarity you decide to use need not be something strikingly obvious to others, but a feature immediately noticeable to you to enable an association with the person's name to be formed. Although word association or correlation will be covered elsewhere, it is also necessary to approach it here as the method can be used to help when trying to remember names.

Being reminded of a name by something completely unrelated is quite a common phenomenon. We often employ the use of objects to help us to remember someone's name. When I was a child, I could never remember the name of the little boy who sat next to me on the bus. I used the word BAT followed by MAT to recollect his name, which was MATHEW. How I arrived at that conclusion after beginning with the word BAT, I shall never know. The important point is that it worked for me, and does so for many people.

Correlating Intermediates

To place two totally unconnected ideas in the memory in such a way that one will immediately recall the other, it is necessary to interject intermediates to link the extremes together. Although you may perceive this practice as being somewhat fanciful, it is a method that most people have used, perhaps without even realising it.

For instance, when trying with no avail to recall the name of Mr Blackburn, you may allow various associated ideas to pass through the mind in the hope that one of them will suggest it. You might begin with Oak tree, then Burning oak, and find the name Blackburn.

Perhaps the name Johnson evades you. If so, the same procedure should be followed: Daughter, Son and John's son, giving you Johnson. However, a fairly reasonable memory is needed to enable you to reach the final conclusion of the name simply by using associated words. But when you also note and employ an obvious peculiarity you know the person has – whether it is a facial feature or even their job – the analysis becomes far easier. Moreover, the use of this method also helps in the long-term to strengthen the natural memory, eventually making recalling names a less arduous task.

Let us suppose that the person whose name you wish to remember is a plumber. He is called Mr Burns. The word 'Plumber' does not in any way suggest the name. Instead, place his job under the heading 'Peculiarity'. Beneath another heading – 'Correlation' – insert Pipe, Smoke and Fire, eventually arriving at the name of Mr Burns. It is fairly easy to see how this conclusion is reached: one word simply suggests another.

These are just examples. You must create your own, so write out a table of as many as you can think of. I will begin with a few more examples. After these, see if you can place the correlated intermediates between the two extremes, thus linking them together.

Peculiarity	Correlation	Name
Barman	Gill, Water	Mr Finn
Small man	Snow-white, Happy	Mr Smiley
Pointed nose	Ink, Pen	Mr Nibbs
Accountant	Bill, Phone, Ring	Mrs Bell
Fat red face		Mr Hampshire
Policeman		Mr Clay
Bushy eyebrows		Mrs Lane
Bright red hair		Miss Bingle
Bank clerk		Mr Harris
Receptionist		Miss Lamb
Fat bald head		Mr Grace
Doctor		Dr Abbot
Nurse		Miss Little
Traffic warden		Mr Jones
Man with limp		Mr David
Eyebrows together		Mr Downley
Protruding teeth		Mrs Ludlow
Miserable face		Miss Phillips
Large eyes		Mrs Ginson
Thin lips		Miss Hedley
Gardener		Mr Smithson
Solicitor		Miss Hughes
Politician		Mr Webb

If you found it difficult creating the appropriate intermediates, make a further list using your own peculiarities and names until you grasp exactly how it is done. With practise, you will become proficient at interjecting the correct words to link the extremes together. The primary advantage of this technique is most certainly the development of the natural memory. Thinking carefully about the intermediates encourages your powers of observation and helps you to pay more attention to detail.

The more observant you become, the greater your capacity for putting names to faces, thus saving you from familiar embarrassing situations of not being able to remember someone's name. This is extremely important and offers many advantages in the business world. But you must also appreciate that no technique is a substitute for a capable natural memory. However, if you use this system regularly, such development will take place. A little effort is all that is needed for the system really to work for you.

It is also important to treat your memory with respect. Always ask it to help you by telling you what it knows. Exercise greatly improves the memory. The intermediates should be recited backwards and forwards from memory to help strengthen their impression and to stop the mind from wandering. Continuity, too, is greatly improved once the correlated intermediates have been firmly cemented in the mind.

This method can be used to recall and learn all kinds of facts, from remembering people's names to mastering a foreign language. Apart from being an efficient system, it is extremely easy to understand. It is also useful for memorising unconnected items. This will be covered in the following chapter.

One of the most important points to remember when endeavouring to recall names is to make the first impression very strong and firmly embedded in the mind. Apart from placing attention upon the person's most obvious characteristic or peculiarity, as already advised listen to the name when it is given. If necessary, ask for it to be repeated. Do not be afraid to show that you are interested in what is being said to you. Occasionally, the characteristic or peculiarity may be quite obvious, immediately bringing to mind a definite connection with someone's name. Once you have grasped the concept of this method, you will not only be able to store an abundance of information in the memory, but also have a lot of fun using it. Practise on everyone you meet.

We sometimes find ourselves trying to recall a person's name because we recognise the way they walk or their clothes. It may well be that how they look at you is familiar and causes you to search your memory for their name. How many times have you found yourself saying 'It's on the tip of my tongue' simply because you cannot put a name to a face? Most people know just how frustrating that can be. Paradoxically, it often seems that the harder we try to think of someone's name, the more it escapes us.

To develop perfect recall, it is important to look upon every thing and every one as having some importance. In other words, you must discipline your mind and cultivate the habit of paying attention to all that you meet. I appreciate that for some people this is difficult, but it is a prerequisite of a good memory.

Finally, create your own peculiarities from this list of names. Using your imagination, think of suitable correlated intermediates with which to unify the peculiarities with the names. Experimentation is extremely important until you discover exactly how it is to be done.

Miss Phipps; Mr Shanks; Mrs Glover; Mr Robinson; Miss Shine; Mr Gee; Miss Green; Miss Ginley; Mrs McDermot; Mrs Forshaw; Mr Mallon; Miss Letterbourgh; Mrs Swift; Mrs Downing; Miss Farrington; Mr Brownlow; Miss Rahman; Mrs Derrylyn; Mrs Townley; Miss Rowe; Mrs Loxey; Miss Liver; Mr Bottomley; Miss Cowley; Miss Boxer; Mrs Pie; Mr French; Mrs Baldwin; Miss Rowan; Mrs Townsend; Mr Dogley; Mrs Doogle; Miss Patel; Miss Polo; Mrs Locke; Mrs Jones; Mr Bennett; Miss Little; Mrs Riddle; Mrs Downing; Miss Kettle; Mrs Kitchener; Mrs Li; Mr Grenyer; Mrs Sawyer; Mr Curb; Miss Lightbody; Mr Lowerhill; Mrs Foot; Miss Hand; Miss Biggley; Mr Farr; Mrs Short; Mr Britain; Miss West; Mrs Walls; Mr Orange; Mrs Southley; Miss Head; Mr Tozzer; Mr Baker; Mrs Crawley; Miss Pinhead; Mr Nail; Miss Letterman; Mrs Bright; Mr Harris; Miss Walker; Mrs Lynch; Mr Dow; Miss Jaffa; Mrs Burns; Miss Cotton; Mr Wenton; Mrs Heinz; Miss Shoeman; Miss Binks; Miss Macniff; Mr Bumble; Mrs Boyle; Mrs Royal; Mr Hill; Miss Settle; Mrs Wilson; Mrs Williamson; Mr Donald; Miss Bootle; Mrs Eden; Mr Dent; Miss Lane; Mrs Rattle; Mr Carr; Miss Rene; Mr Carter; Mrs Phillips; Mr Donovan; Mrs Baxter; Mrs Long; Mr Dimond; Mrs Sowter; Mr Howard; Miss Shaw; Mr Ocean; Mr Black; Mrs Simpson; Miss Kite; Mrs Flynn; Mrs White; Mr Dunn; Mrs London.

Be as adventurous as you like in your choice of intermediates. Allow your mind to explore every scenario to create the peculiarities and characteristics. If you take your time when studying the names, you will find yourself becoming proficient at linking the extremes together. The object of the exercise is to learn to remember names and faces.

6

Memorising Unconnected Items

When your work involves much mental activity and necessitates an efficient memory, remembering long lists can be arduous enough without having to recall lots of details which are completely unrelated to each other. Using intermediates is not only an extremely effective way of accomplishing such an arduous task, but the exercise can also prove to be a lot of fun.

Some memory experts often refer to the process of linking two unrelated words together as 'Catenation', derived from the Latin word *catena*, meaning 'Chain'. As we know, a chain is composed of a varying number of links. In the same way, Catenation connects two completely unrelated ideas with the use of intermediates. This unifying process can also be of enormous help when learning a foreign language, and will assist you when there is a problem remembering certain words. Once the method has been mastered, you should find it an invaluable aid to remembering unrelated ideas and words.

As we learned previously, the two opposing or unrelated words are 'extremes' whilst the unifying words become 'intermediates'. With this process, it is possible to connect words that have no relation whatsoever, such as Horse and Sky. These two extremes may be united by interjecting the intermediates *Head* and *Overhead*, thus presenting the complete Catenation: Horse – *head* – *overhead* – Sky.

Catenation also dispenses with the traditional shopping list by allowing you to commit to memory all the products to purchase. Using this method, there is no limit to the items that can be memorised. But before employing Catenation, there are a few important facts to remember:

a) Each intermediate should take you farther away from the first extreme and nearer to the last.

b) Try not to use more intermediates than needed.

c) It should never be necessary to employ over three intermediates. In most cases two – or even one – will suffice. It is far better to use single words as intermediates since double words may cause complications.

Creating a Catenation

Creating a Catenation varies from person to person as it depends upon individual perception. One earlier memory expert gave examples of what intermediates different people would use in creating a Catenation. The extremes he cited as examples were Hands and Destiny. To connect these two words – thus creating the first Catenation – a philosopher would probably use the intermediates Clock, Time and Eternity. The complete Catenation would then read 'Hands – *clock – time – eternity* – Destiny'.

It was suggested that a Socialist might employ the intermediates *Grasping, Capitalism* and *Socialism*, making the complete Catenation read 'Hands – *Grasping – Capitalism – Socialism* – Destiny'. Finally, he suggested a woman would be more practical and to the point, using only one intermediate – *Palmistry*. The complete Catenation would then read 'Hands – *Palmistry* – Destiny'.

How to Use a Catenation

Make certain that the Catenation is fixed solidly in the mind and that you can recite it off by heart. Firstly, insert the appropriate intermediates between the two extremes – the words you need to connect– and include the whole Catenation in a mental analysis to help you to fix the true nature of the connections in the memory. Then mentally recite the intermediates backwards and forwards until you are quite certain they can be recalled without effort. Excluding the intermediates completely, conclude the mental exercise by repeating the two extremes together from memory by themselves. This process should be repeated until you can recite the whole Catenation from memory without any trouble.

When you find some words completely resistant to recall, creating a Catenation somehow sets the memory's programme into motion, allowing an obstinate memory to be overcome. You will be surprised just how quickly this method of memory recall can be learned. Once adopted, it is extremely important to revive it every so often to avoid the danger of losing it before it has produced the desired results.

When a positive connection has been established between the two extremes, the intermediates will no longer be required. Having served their purpose, they may fade completely from the memory. The mind then creates its own connection between the two extremes, allowing the intermediates to be free for use in the unification of other words.

Most people who claim a poor memory have simply not learned to file the information in the correct compartment. The memory is a mental filing cabinet in which everything is properly stored in either numerical or alphabetical order. When you misfile information, it becomes extremely difficult to find. You will eventually recover it, but it takes longer, calling for much more effort. In order to develop and cultivate a capable memory, you must begin by tidying your mind, rearranging thoughts so that you know exactly where to find them.

When the mind is presented with a group of unconnected ideas, it encounters difficulty recalling them instantly. The inability to integrate what it perceives arises from the fact that there is no order or similarity. However, when a means of grammatical arrangement is introduced, the mind is able to perceive the individual components as one integrated whole. To achieve this simply rearrange the unconnected ideas so that they form some semblance of order and association. Now study the following list of words. See how many you can write down from memory in the correct order:

CHIMNEY	GARDEN
GUITAR	STUDENT
SPECTACLES	DOOR
DOG	BOTTLE
COLLEGE	VILLAGE
VAN	PEN
OLD LADY	HOUSE
TREE	MILK

You probably did not do as well as you hoped. This time, try to rearrange the words so that one relates in some way to the other.

Follow the same procedure. I have listed them in a connected order to give some idea of how to go about it:

VILLAGE	*GUITAR*
HOUSE	*PEN*
CHIMNEY	*BOTTLE*
DOOR	*MILK*
GARDEN	*VAN*
TREE	*OLD LADY*
COLLEGE	*SPECTACLES*
STUDENT	*DOG*

The first list illustrates just how difficult it is to remember unconnected ideas. If you rearranged the words so that one held an association to the next, you should have found that each one automatically suggested the other, and so on. The secret of an efficient memory is in your ability to place items in order. Details that follow in sequence are far easier to remember than those that do not.

Most people can recite the alphabet from beginning to end, but only those who have practised can do so in reverse without any difficulty. Although we can all deliver the alphabet without any trouble, we have to maintain the rhythm to help us follow the correct sequence. Should we be interrupted for some reason or other, we usually have to flick mentally through all the letters before we can continue. Sequences and patterns are therefore easier than disordered items to remember. A tidy thinker usually possesses a good and capable memory.

One of the main reasons for not being able to remember unconnected details is that our psychological conditioning allows us only to recall items that are orderly and uniform. We are not mentally prepared for the unexpected. Unless our work involves having to remember more than one thing at a time, it is highly unlikely that our memories will work as well as they should.

I am confident that everyone has the potential to cultivate a good memory – and all it takes is a little concentrated effort and a tidier approach to the way you think.

When faced with several unconnected matters to remember, place them in order or some semblance of sequence before storing them in the memory. It may well be that as you work your way through this programme you will discover ways of creating your own methods of memory recall. That is the system to employ as long as it works and produces exactly the results you require.

In business, forgetfulness is extremely irritating – not to mention costly – especially when it results in the loss of a contract because of a missed appointment. Being in commerce can be very stressful: even when an appointment is entered in the diary, it may still be overlooked. This might happen regardless of whether or not someone has a bad memory.

Even businessmen with good memories frequently forget important appointments. A person with a bad one will usually forget completely whereas those with a good memory only do so when something out of the ordinary suddenly happens to over-ride the appointment or detail that was to be remembered. This can easily happen with an extremely active and busy mind.

Preparing the Mental Diary
Firstly, a more systematic focusing of the attention is needed when involved in the world of business. On the days when you have more than one important appointment, keep fixing the word 'TIME' firmly in your mind. Use your watch as the mental key to remind you.

It may not be possible to remember all your meetings, especially when you are occupied with a vital conference or involved in something that needs your total attention. Conditioning yourself constantly to check your watch is an ideal way of precipitating the memory. Although far more effective, checking your watch is like tying a piece of cotton to your finger to remind you to do something. It is quite possible to place yourself on automatic pilot – as it were – so you go through the motions of your daily routine almost mechanically whilst still subconsciously focused on other tasks that have to be done later.

Training yourself this way creates an inner alarm clock. With practise, regardless of what you are doing, you will find yourself being called to time as you suddenly remember exactly what it is you have to do.

Creating that Inner Clock
All you need to create a subconscious clock is to spend five minutes sitting quietly every morning before leaving for work.

Relax in a comfortable chair, with your eyes closed and the spine straight. Focus your attention to the tip of your nose. Imagine you can see the face of a large clock in front of you. Picture it very clearly in your mind. Note the figures and hands moving slowly around the circumference.

Breathe rhythmically until the rhythm is fully established, allowing the inhalations and exhalations to be slow and evenly spaced.

Allow the clock face to appear very bright. See it pulsating and glowing in your mind.

Only be conscious of the numbers 12, 6, 3 and 9. Look upon these figures as being the keys to your punctuality and the most important in the clock's numerical sequence. Whilst focusing your attention totally upon the clock face, continue to breathe rhythmically. Every time you inhale, allow another figure to appear on the face. Begin with the number 1, exhale, then the number 2, exhale, next 3, exhale, etc.

When the clock's numerical sequence has been completed, allow the times of your appointments for that day to be brought to mind, beginning with the earliest.

Should the first one be at 11 am, focus your attention for a few moments on that numerical point on the clock. Whilst breathing slowly and deeply, allow that figure to disappear. Continue to breathe rhythmically for a few moments longer before permitting the figure 11 to reappear. Follow this with your next appointment, for example 2 pm, and repeat the process. Should you have another meeting for 3.30 pm, focus the attention upon the figure 3. This makes it less complicated and will still produce the correct results. Complete your diary of appointments for the day, then very slowly close the clock down completely. This may also be practised at night, in preparation for the following day, then repeated again before leaving for work.

It would be silly to disregard this particular exercise until you have at least given it a chance. It may take a little while before the programme has been created and the subconscious mind fully absorbs it. Once achieved, you will be surprised at the results. Conclude the practice with slow, rhythmic breathing. This will help to clear and prepare the mind for the day. There is no better way of encouraging the memory to produce that which we require.

Throughout the day, use the word 'TIME' as your mantra. Now and again, silently intonate it to reinforce your connection with the last exercise. Touch your wrist-watch with the index and second fingers simultaneously with the intonation to help set your programme in motion.

When engrossed in a project or tied up with a business meeting and you know you have an appointment in the next hour or so, touch your watch and silently say 'TIME'. If alone, close your eyes for a moment and see the clock in your mind.

This exercise may be integrated into any other memory programme you happen to be using and will serve you as a mental discipline, helping to encourage your concentration. Used over long periods, there is little doubt in my mind that this method of visualisation will aid memory improvement immensely.

More Correlations: Connected Ideas

The process of remembering connected words is followed in exactly the same way as unconnected words. When the memory is poor, even the simplest of words can be a chore to recall so a little assistance is needed.

This, as we have already discussed, is done with the aid of a Correlation consisting of one or more unifying intermediates. Whether the words or ideas are connected or not, the intermediates glue them together to make a lasting impression upon the memory.

A journey to the shops to purchase food for an evening meal can be a nuisance, particularly when there are so many other tasks to undertake during the day. Fish, sauce, potatoes, salad, wine and wine glasses can easily be written on a list along with the other things that you need to do or purchase.

However, a capable, meticulous mind can quite easily commit these matters – and more – to memory with the simple process of correlating intermediates. However, you must understand the Laws of Association and exactly how these can work for you when endeavouring to bring two ideas together with the use of one or more words.

As explained, the two ideas you are seeking to unify are referred to as 'Extremes' whilst the words that have been correlated to cement them together in the memory are called 'Intermediates'.

Write the word 'Extreme' twice on a piece of paper in the following way, and 'Intermediates' in between.

Extreme	Intermediates	Extreme
Fish	Dish, Spoon	Sauce
Potatoes	Salad cream	Salad
Wine	Bottle, Cork	Wineglasses

Again, these are just examples to give you an idea. Try interjecting intermediates in the following.

Extreme	Intermediates	Extreme
Writing pad		Ruler
Cotton wool		Lipstick
Apples		Oranges
Tea-bags		Milk
Tie		Shirt
Curtains		Window cleaner
Light bulb		Lamp shade
Shampoo		Hairbrush
Shoes		Socks
Diary		Address book
Envelopes		Stamps
Hammer		Saw
Wallpaper		Paint
Mirror		Dusters
Air-freshener		Furniture polish
Trousers		Jumper
Bread		Cheese
Dictionary		Pens
Flowers		Vase
Perfume		Soap

Try not to disregard these examples because of their simplistic appearance. They have been given only as an exercise in imagination and to see how quickly you can create the connection between the two extremes. You should be surprised with your ability to unify the two extremes, even though the two have a direct connection and relationship with each other.

The important point to remember when creating intermediates is to use your imagination as much as possible. As long as the word or words you interject lead you directly to the final extreme, they are the correct ones to use.

The whole programme is designed to aid the cultivation of your natural memory and to precipitate your true mental potential. If you desperately want to have an incredible memory and to be able to remember almost anything at all, you need to follow the programme through from beginning to end. *Do not dismiss anything in the book without putting it to the test. Do not try to take in too much at any one time.*

Have a break. Give yourself time to digest what you have already learned. Read the book through once before even attempting any of the exercises and techniques. Take time with each chapter. Practise as much as possible. This system of word association helps the memory immensely to overcome laziness and teaches the mind to be focused. With increased use of your creative abilities the memory will become sharper. Adopting Catenation aids the subconscious mind to make the appropriate connections between ideas and facilitates memory recall.

To put your powers of association to the test, study the next list of words and write down the first word that comes into your mind. Do not spend too much time studying the list. Simply read through it once, then write down the words you associate with those in the list. Again, try not to spend too much time thinking about the words as the idea is to act spontaneously, thus putting your powers of imagination to the test. Try this first exercise just to see how well you do.

Do not have a negative attitude and say, 'I can't do that! I do not have a good imagination'. Everyone has an imagination. Even a poor one can be improved upon whilst a good one can be made even better with use.

BALL; NEEDLE; TREE; SHIP; NOSE; SHOE; CAR; BOY; STREET-LAMP; CLOUD; GUN; COAT; COW; FENCE; STAMP; PEN; RAIN; MAP; TABLE; HANDBAG; BIBLE; FIREPLACE; DOOR; TELEVISION; PHOTOGRAPH;

MIRROR; TOY; BOOK; CANDLE; ROAD; WINE; WAR; SAILOR; HOLE; MOUNTAIN; SNOW; RAIN; ICE-CREAM; COAL; SWEETS; WINDOW; APPLE; GARDEN; SOCKS.

See how well you did. Do not be too disheartened if the results are not what you expected. Now repeat the process once more and note if there is any improvement in the time it takes. When you have done this, spend no more than two minutes studying the next list. Using the method of association that you have hopefully learned in this chapter, try to remember the words in the correct sequence.

Again, do not dwell on the individual words too long as the most effective way to fix them in the memory is to allow your eyes slowly to scan the lines, mentally absorbing no more than six words at a time. Once you have mastered memorising the words in the correct order, attempt to remember them in reverse:

CAT; CARPET; HOUSE; RADIO; CAR; AEROPLANE; TREE; DOLL; BOTTLE; TABLE; TIN; VASE; ORNAMENT; ENVELOPE; PEN; SPECTACLE; NEEDLE; TELEPHONE; PAPER CLIP; TELEVISION; PHOTOGRAPH; CANDLE; TABLE; BIRD; PLANT; SHIRT; BOOK; RING; NAIL.

Do not be too adventurous at the beginning. Mentally break the words up into groups of six. Memorised in this way, you will find them much easier to visualise and lodge in the memory. It is a good idea to repeat this exercise a few times before moving to the next part.

Carefully study the following list. In the spaces, write in a word which you think will lead one to the other. Study the list for no longer than one minute. Think carefully about the word you believe will make a good unifying intermediate. Some words are connected whilst others are not. You may have to employ two intermediates to unify the two extremes: use whatever you feel is necessary to create a Catenation. After this list, I have given some examples of words I feel make effective intermediates. Try not to look at mine until you have completed your insertions.

BALL	—	BAT
APPLE	—	ORANGE
PIN	—	CUSHION

TEARS	—	SADNESS
FIREPLACE	—	MAT
GOLDFISH	—	COOKER
TABLECLOTH	—	JUG
PURSE	—	SHOE
MOUSE	—	WINDOWSILL
BOAT	—	MOUNTAIN
GLUE	—	NEWSPAPER
CALENDAR	—	STATUE
CAMERA	—	PARK
SWAN	—	POLICEMAN
CHAIR	—	DOG
LIGHT	—	LEMON
TIN	—	JAR
LOVE	—	TOUCH
STAMP	—	BOX
BANANA	—	CAKE
CLOCK	—	HAND
SKETCH PAD	—	SOLDIER
HANDBAG	—	SCISSORS
TYPEWRITER	—	BOW
WEDDING CAKE	—	WINE
COMB	—	BEACH
PUPPY DOG	—	PRIVATE INVESTIGATOR

Use whatever is necessary if you feel that you need more than one intermediate to unify the two extremes.

BALL – *HIT* – BAT; APPLE – *PIP* – ORANGE; PIN – *COTTON* – CUSHION; TEARS – *CRY* –SADNESS; FIREPLACE – *HEARTH* – MAT; GOLDFISH – *BOWL* – COOKER; TABLE-CLOTH – *TABLE* – JUG; PURSE – *LACE* – SHOE; MOUSE – *CAT* – WINDOW-SILL; BOAT – *HORIZON* – MOUN-TAIN; GLUE – *PASTE* – NEWSPAPER; CALENDAR – *FIGURE* – STATUE; CAMERA – *PHOTOGRAPH* – *FAMILY* – PARK; SWAN – *LAKE* – *PARK* – POLICEMAN; CHAIR – *LEG* – *WALK* – DOG; LIGHT – *CAKE* – LEMON; TIN – *POLISH* –*JAM* – JAR; LOVE – *KISS* – *CARESS* – TOUCH; STAMP – *CHRISTMAS* – BOX; BANANA – *PIE* – *FRUIT* – CAKE; CLOCK – *FINGER*

– HAND; SKETCH PAD – *PLAN* – SOLDIER; HANDBAG – *NAIL-FILE* –
SCISSORS; TYPEWRITER – *RIBBON* – BOW; WEDDING CAKE – *TOAST*
– WINE; COMB – *SAND* – BEACH; PUPPY DOG – *LEAD* – PRIVATE
INVESTIGATOR.

You will probably find that this exercise stretches the imagination
and helps to focus the attention. If you truly want to develop an
extremely good memory with perfect recall, this method should be
practised frequently until you become accustomed to the art of
spontaneously creating words with which to unify the two extremes.
Try to find words to associate with everything you do and see.
Mentally link together all the objects around you. Practise word association at every chance. Create an association with every thing and
every one with whom you come into contact and exercise your mind.

7
The Story System

Even for someone with a reasonably good memory, remembering long lists is a chore. But for anyone with a bad one, such a task may be a near impossibility. Of course, we can use any of the systems previously given to aid us in our efforts to remember or even to help overcome absent mindedness. However, unless there is a systematic approach to the way in which data is stored in the memory, I am afraid that all our efforts would simply be in vain.

We usually have no trouble recollecting events that have interested us. The mind recalls of its own accord memories of both sadness and happiness. We are sometimes forced to deal with a reoccurring memory of a past traumatic experience. This may be triggered by something we subconsciously associate with that particular episode.

The same applies to memories of happy events. These are recalled quite easily along with great warmth and emotion. It would appear that we have no control whatsoever over such memories, but they very often exert great control over us. Events that have passed by almost unnoticed are more difficult to recollect. Even when we try to remember them, they seem to sink deeper into the dark depths of the subconscious. This proves that a strong first impression most certainly must be made to enable the memory to be accessed easily.

The subconscious mind represents an extremely complex area of our psychological make-up. I believe we are no nearer now to understanding it than we were at the beginning of the century. Of one aspect we can rest assured: the subconscious can be entered and encouraged to produce secrets it so desperately tries to conceal.

The simpler the approach, the better the results. Presenting the mind with an idea to which it relates and also associates with another idea is very often all that is needed to encourage it to reveal what it knows. Of all memory recall methods, the Story System is perhaps the easiest of all to learn and use.

It involves creating a scenario around what you need to remember. Most people can remember a story. But by weaving the details you need to recall into a story line they can easily be called upon when needed. As the story is created by you, it can follow any theme you choose. You may even select an episode from your life as a story line. Include as many things you need to remember as you like.

Trying to memorise long lists can be difficult for most people, but by creating a story around them they become far easier to recall. The story can be serious or even have a ridiculous theme. As long as it helps you to find exactly what you need to remember, the nature of the plot is not really that important. The primary point to be considered when endeavouring to create a good story line is to take care where and how you place the details.

Position them strategically throughout the story, but try to avoid having them too close together. Be as consistent as possible with the story line, ensuring it is easy to follow. Avoid making it too complicated as this causes confusion and makes it difficult to remember.

A good, strong story line may be used time and time again. Although the plot could remain the same, the details you need to remember can be changed as often as necessary. Let us take a look at a few examples of how to create a story. Try to use your imagination, allowing your creative skills to guide you. Be as imaginative as possible, keeping characters down to a minimum to facilitate recall.

Story Example One

Let us suppose that you are on a business trip to a different part of the country. On the train, you realise you have left your notes behind. These are extremely important as they list items to bring up at the business meeting to which you are travelling.

Overwhelmed by panic, you find yourself trying mentally to recall all the details. Although you can write them down, you know full well that you desperately need to commit them to memory to make them have more of an impact. Having considered the list very carefully, the topics you must remember are: A new car; American business trip; annual pay; moving home; the opening of a new factory; the retirement of John Smithdown; the lighting outside the factory; employing more staff.

These topics are not so straight forward that a story can be created without careful thought. The plot needs to be considered to enable the main points to be clearly defined throughout. The object is to facilitate recall. If the points to be remembered have not been carefully placed, they will not impress the memory sufficiently to be recalled. The main details must sparkle to make them stand out and impress the memory.

To make the story work successfully for you, it is essential to secure it sufficiently and firmly in the mind so that you know it from beginning to end. If the story is quite familiar you should have no problem memorising it. However, if it is one you have formulated especially, you must make that extra effort to learn it. Let us now take a look at creating a story. This is just to give you an idea of how the items you need to remember can be placed strategically.

Story

John Smithdown was looking forward so much to his *retirement* at the end of the month. Whenever he thought about not having to get up at the same time every morning, a smile of satisfaction dawned across his face. He just could not believe that the company had given him a *new car* as a retirement present. He always promised himself an up-to-date model, but knew only too well that his *annual pay* would not have allowed this. Now he and his wife could take that *American trip*. They would also have far more time to spend together.

John Smithdown had always been a very down-to-earth, practical man. Never out of work since fifteen, he was now looking forward to the rest of his life. Both he and his wife Jean planned to *move home*, perhaps to a bungalow in the country, nearer to their daughter. Anyway, they would have to vacate the company house as that accompanied the job. John Smithdown smiled as he climbed into his new car. He was so proud to have been associated with such a big company, which had already opened a *new factory* and now begun to increase their *work force*.

It was not until John Smithdown reached the same gates he had driven through for forty-five years that he noticed *new lighting* had been installed. Well, perhaps it was time to hang up his security uniform for the very last time, he thought to himself.

Stories are fairly easy to remember. Most people can recall the tales of 'Little Red Riding Hood', 'Alice in Wonderland' or even the complex story line of Charles Dickens' 'Christmas Carol'. Though perhaps not remembering the exact details, the general theme is often recalled with ease.

Stories are easily planted in the mind, but make the tale interesting so it has a strong and vivid impression upon the subconscious. The sillier it is, the greater the impact on the memory. Creating unusual and humorous scenarios around details to remember is often the most effective way of securing them in the mind. Even unconnected matters can quite easily be recalled simply by weaving them into the main structure of a story. Individual objects may slip from the memory. Once fixed, stories very rarely do.

Try not to be too dismissive of the Story System simply because it appears somewhat childish. As long as there is a consistent theme running through the story from beginning to end, it should be fairly simple to follow and therefore remember. Even a long shopping list can be included. As well as being an extremely effective method of remembering, this system is amusing to use.

It may be dismissed on the grounds that it is quicker and much more practical to write things down. It is probably far easier, but this lazy approach does not do an awful lot for the general improvement of the natural memory. Writing matters to remember on a piece of paper can be likened to travelling everywhere in your motor car. This does not do anything to exercise the body, eventually causing muscles to waste away.

Similarly, the memory becomes ineffective through lack of use. Setting a task by involving it in some mental activity facilitates recall, and in the long term aids general efficiency. The primary object of this memory programme is to improve the functioning of the natural memory, not to offer the easier option of writing everything down.

Story Example Two

Shopping is one of those necessary jobs we all have to do, whether we like it or not. However, the Story System can make it more fun and help to improve the natural memory in the process.

Instead of relying upon pieces of paper to remind you of purchases, create a simple story around them. In this busy and hectic life it is all too easy to forget things you need so desperately to do. When rushed off your feet with so much to think about, you may become overwhelmed by stress, even to the extent that you forget exactly why you went to the shops!

Creating a story is perhaps the safest way of fixing something in your mind. Very little effort is needed to remember a story, particularly one that holds the interest and can present all the matters we need to recall.

Let us suppose that a dinner party arranged at the last minute forces you to dash into town before the shops close. Driving through the rush hour traffic, you are mentally preparing the list of all the goods you need – chicken, potatoes, vegetables, fruit, a selection of cheeses, fresh cream, French bread, wine and napkins. The story goes like this:

Little Alice followed her curiosity once again through the door that had previously led her into another time. Upon reaching the other side she was immediately overwhelmed by the bright colours. Everything looked so huge and out of proportion in comparison to her small and slightly built figure.

The sight of a giant *chicken* coming towards Alice caught her attention. This was no ordinary *chicken*, for it was bright pink and beckoned for Alice to follow. It led her into a beautiful garden where she was amazed to see the tallest *fruit* trees she had ever encountered in her life – *bananas, apples, pears, oranges, plums* and *melons*.

In the far corner of the garden, Alice noticed the largest, funniest *vegetables* ever – *lettuces, broccoli, peas, cucumbers and cabbages*, and many more she had never seen before. These were no ordinary vegetables, for they could talk and all shouted 'Hello Alice!' She smiled with delight as the giant *chicken* led her towards a table neatly laid with all manner of food and drink.

Seated around it were funny little creatures, all wearing party hats. 'Pour Alice a glass of *wine*,' said one of the strange-looking guests. 'I'm too young to drink *wine*,' grinned Alice. 'Anyway, it is horrible.'

By now, Alice was hungry and her eyes scanned the table for something to eat. To her horror, she saw a huge piece of green and mouldy *cheese* crawling with maggots. 'How horrible!' exclaimed Alice. 'I can't eat that!'

'Why not?' asked one of the funny creatures. 'It's absolutely delicious.'

'Then you eat it,' added Alice. 'I'll just have a piece of *French bread* and some *fresh cream*.' As Alice reached across the table, she noticed huge jacket *potatoes*, hot and delicious. 'I'll have one of these,' she said, placing it neatly on the plate in front of her. 'And I'll have another one to take home with me.' Alice took a *napkin* and folded it neatly around the hot *potato*.

'You are home,' interrupted one of the funny creatures. 'You are home.'

Alice opened her eyes to the sound of the alarm clock ringing. 'Time to get up for school,' she yawned. 'It was all a dream.'

This is certainly not an example of every day life, but an ideal way of helping to cement unconnected items in the mind. The sillier the story, the better it will be in achieving this.

Remember that the story can follow any theme you like and be as ridiculous as you want. Think about the plot and the theme very carefully. Place the points to be remembered strategically throughout the scenario. It is also important that there is consistency, and that the items you need to recollect do not appear out of context. Integrate them carefully so that the story makes a greater impression.

Use the following words around which to create a story of your own. Allow a little freedom to be given to your imagination, making the story line as crazy and surreal as possible. The tale does not really have to make a great deal of sense as long as it is one that can be easily fixed in the mind. The primary object of this system is to help you remember specific items so base the account solely upon them. Obviously, it is more difficult to weave a story around a long list. To make the system effective, keep the salient objects or items to a minimum. You may have difficulty remembering more than twenty at one time, though it is not entirely impossible. You can always choose to use one of the other memory systems given later.

Make the theme a walk in the countryside. The points you need to remember are: Mountain bike; eggs; glue; tape measure; shampoo; pair of socks; mirror; envelopes; furniture polish and washing up liquid.

A country walk is possibly not the ideal theme for a story considering all the different points you need to recall, but this combination will most certainly make you think whilst using your creative abilities. Try not to make it too crowded. Think carefully about how best to place the listed items for maximum effect – and make the story work for you.

If you have an inability to visualise, you may initially encounter some difficulty creating the correct story around the details you need to remember. Someone who is not naturally creative will have to put a little more effort into visualisation. However, the imagery faculty can be encouraged and precipitated with a few simple exercises to improve concentration and the ability to focus. Visualisation is essential in the cultivation of an efficient memory, especially when systems such as the Story method are employed.

Should concentration be one of your main problems, the ability to focus the mind must be the primary aim. Creating a story around matters you need to remember is an ideal way of aiding the memory's development. The techniques given in the following chapter will also enhance your ability to visualise and recall.

If the memory is not used to its fullest possible potential, it becomes sluggish. Using the imagery faculty in the process of visualisation precipitates the memory and aids retention. People with poor memories usually lack concentration and are not very observant. Their ability to recall is inefficient, so quite often the mind falls into the habit of not being able to remember. In a way, I suppose this is due to self-conditioning or self-programming, as it is often called. But let me stress that the memory *can* be re-programmed to help it to produce the necessary data.

8

Focusing and Visualisation

As explained, the memory can be greatly improved with the use of specific visualisation techniques. These simple methods not only aid the cultivation of the imagery faculty – necessary in the process of seeing in the mind's eye – but the concentration also benefits, too. A person who has no difficulty visualising would probably not understand the reasons why others cannot do so.

Many people find it almost impossible to create and see mental pictures. For them, it is difficult to comprehend how visualisation occurs. But everyone *can* visualise, to a greater or lesser degree. All it takes is practise with the correct technique.

Should the phenomenon of visualisation be hard for you to master, you would find it impossible to create a picture in the mind of anything you cannot see and touch. Therefore, the first step must be to encourage the image-making faculty by presenting something concrete upon which to focus. It is essential to impress the mind sufficiently to cause a clear mental image to appear before it.

Step One

We have all experienced the optical phenomenon resulting from looking into an extremely bright light, such as a camera flash. When the lens of the eye is shocked, an after-image is created within the image-making faculty of the mind. This usually remains for a few seconds before finally becoming fragmented and disappearing completely.

To try this experiment, you will need a lighted candle and a comfortable chair.

For maximum results, the exercise is best followed in a darkened room. Place the lighted candle as near to eye level as possible, approximately three feet away from where you are sitting. It is important to keep the spine straight whilst remaining relaxed. Place your hands comfortably on your lap, fixing your gaze gently on the flame.

The object of the exercise is to impress the lens of the eye sufficiently to cause an image to form in the mind. Simply look at the
flame, resisting all temptation to move your stare away, even for a
moment. Try not to blink. Allow your gaze to be fixed at the tip of
the flame. Follow this process for approximately one minute, but
longer if possible.

During the process of gazing at the flame, try not to think of any
one particular matter. Do not impose any restrictions upon your
thoughts.

Step Two
When your eyes begin to tear and smart and you absolutely cannot
continue, close them very slowly. Place the palms of your hands over
your eyes, applying a little pressure as you do so.

Within moments, the after-image of the flame will appear in the
mind's eye. Try to hold it for as long as you possibly can by exerting
your will and control over it.

It will manifest in the complementary colour of the flame, a sort
of reversed colour. Hold it for as long as possible in your mind. Eventually, it will become fragmented and begin to break up. At this
point, you should open your eyes, return your gaze to the flame and
repeat the process.

Greater control may be exerted over the after-image by
breathing rhythmically i. e. slowly and deeply. The process of concentration often causes breathing to be shallow and irregular. This is
counter-productive and impairs both the concentration and the
memory. Correct breathing is vitally important in the development of
a good memory.

When you have repeated the process of staring three times, the
following process must be practised very carefully.

Step Three
For this part of the exercise, you will also need a one-foot square
piece of white card or fairly thick paper.

Follow the same procedure as you did with the previous step.
Gaze at the candle flame to the point where your eyes begin to
water. Close them for a few moments to establish the after-image in

your mind. When this appears, very slowly open your eyes and move your gaze to the white card, which you should hold in front of you.

Watch the image of the flame being projected onto the card, seeking to keep it in that position for as long as possible. The image will appear translucent and seem to float around in front of you. Using all your will power, try to hold the projected image still and in one place. Exerting your control, seek to move it from side to side, then from corner to corner. Once you are able to do this, your ability to focus and project is starting to develop.

When the projected image begins to fade, return your gaze to the flame and repeat the process. Do so up to five times to ensure that you fully understand the way the technique works.

For the best results, try and practise this exercise every day, or as often as possible. When you feel certain that something positive has developed, you can move to the following step.

Now that you have experienced exactly what it is like to look into the image-making faculty of the mind, we must take the exercise a little further to enable you mentally to explore shape and colour. This experiment encourages the mind's ability to remember and to 'see' exactly what it remembers. With the normal process of remembering, most people have no more than a superficial encounter with their memories. Training the mind mentally to perceive the memories it produces also enables the process of remembering to become more accurate.

The majority of people remember without seeing what they remember. Desperately searching the memory for something in particular becomes far easier when the mental eye is brought into operation. Most individuals put very little effort into the process of remembering. Trying to force a memory to the surface of the mind dissipates force needlessly – and has completely the opposite effect!

For this experiment, draw a circle on a white piece of paper. Draw a dot in the centre of the circle. This is to be the focal point for your concentration and plays an extremely important part in the precipitation of memory and recall.

Sit comfortably as before, placing the circle where you can see it quite clearly. Allow your gaze to be fixed on the dot. Breathe slowly and deeply whilst impressing your mind with the image of the circle.

Resist the temptation to blink or to move your stare away from the circle, even for a moment. When your gaze begins to weaken and your eyes water, close them as before and watch the circle's after-image appear in the mind's eye. This time it is not necessary to place your palms over the eyes. Just sit quietly and see the image in your mind.

When it fades and disappears completely, instead of returning your gaze to the circle on the paper before you, allow your eyes to remain closed. Very slowly, from memory re-create the circle in your mind.

Little effort should be needed mentally to see such a simple shape. Once you have established the circle fully in your mind, imagine the black dot spreading very slowly until the circle is completely covered.

Now picture a round, black shape in your mind, in the centre of which you should create a white dot. Focus on this for a few moments, then visualise it growing and spreading until the entire round image has once again become a white circle. In the centre of the circle, see a black dot for a second time.

As before, focus your attention on the black dot and watch it spreading until the circle is completely black. In the centre of the round, black shape once again imagine a white spot. Following the same procedure as previously, mentally allow the white spot to grow and spread until the round shape has become completely white. This mental process should be repeated several times, or until you tire with the exercise. Follow it meticulously to produce the correct positive results.

Repeating the process teaches the mind to create images and to recall them immediately. Although the circle is an extremely simple shape to imagine, the process of creating the positive and negative images helps to strengthen and improve the natural memory. Though the image is very simple mentally to create, the exercise may need some practise before it is fully understood and achieved. Mental interaction takes place during the process of transferring the positive to the negative, the effects of which are two-fold on the memory. It not only aids your ability mentally to visualise images clearly, but the efficiency of the memory is also improved immensely.

Before the memory can be improved it needs to be organised and tidied, and memories placed in the correct compartments. The simplest visualisation techniques are quite often the most effective. The following system is one which may be in danger of being disregarded completely because of its simplicity, but the Balloon method is one I have used successfully in workshops for a number of years. Coupled with the colours of the spectrum, the Balloon system becomes an extremely effective aid to the memory and the process of recall.

Memory Balloons

Sit in a comfortable armchair, eliminating all distractions to the best of your ability. Breathe rhythmically until the rhythm is fully established, making the mind quiet and serene.

The programme must be prepared before the Balloon method can be used to its full.

Close your eyes. Imagine yourself holding onto the strings of seven large balloons, each in a colour of the spectrum.

Look at each balloon in turn, beginning with the red one. Notice how bright the colours appear. Each balloon pulsates with energy and collectively appears to radiate an intense power that causes you to hold onto the strings tightly.

Make a mental note of how you are affected by each individual colour. Red may engender warmth and strength.

Take a peek at the orange balloon. This colour could fill you with ambition and strength. Next, examine the yellow balloon, which might overwhelm you with a feeling of excitement, making your mind sharp and very clear.

Study the green balloon. This hue may make you calm and reassured. Then the blue balloon appears. It is the shade of blue seen in a clear Summer sky, and probably causes you to feel relaxed, filling you with vitality and power.

Now take a look at the indigo balloon. Perhaps you feel wise, nostalgic and calm. Finally, turn to the violet balloon. You are possibly imbued with a sense of peace and clarity of thought.

Now that you have completed your analysis of the balloons and their colours, you should be ready to move to the following step. But before doing so, it is vital to analyse exactly what effect each colour had upon you.

The Balloon method is extremely simple, and one needing minimum effort. Each coloured balloon represents a day of the week, and collectively serves as a mental diary.

Balloon Exercise
Once the Balloon method has been cultivated and fully established in the subconscious mind, it becomes an invaluable way of reminding you of jobs and duties.

Sit in a comfortable chair, making the mind quiet by breathing rhythmically. Allow the inhalations and exhalations to be evenly spaced. Close your eyes to create a blank screen in your mind.

Gradually let the blank screen come alive. See your seven coloured balloons floating on the air before you.

Each balloon is attached to a piece of string that hangs loosely. Mentally reach out and take the string attached to the red balloon. Slowly draw it towards you.

Focus all your attention on the red balloon. With your finger, mentally write *Sunday* across it. Now release it and watch it float before you.

Do the same with the orange balloon. Mentally take the string in your hand and draw it towards you. Focus all your attention on it for a few moments, then write *Monday* across it. As with the first balloon, let go, watching it float in front of you.

Follow the same procedure with the other balloons, writing across each one the days of the rest of the week. Familiarise yourself with the colours of the balloons and the days they represent, placing these firmly in your mind.

The programme must be established in the following way before the Balloon method can be used successfully.

Programming
Mentally scan through your working week one day at a time. As your thoughts move through each day, focus your attention simultaneously on the corresponding balloon.

On Monday, you may have to call at the bank, collect your suits from the dry-cleaners and pick up a client from the station. Establish these tasks in your mind. Mentally discharge them into the appropriate balloon in the following way.

See the orange balloon very clearly in your mind. Enlarge it so that it is at least four times the size.

In front of the balloon, mentally write in the air *Bank, dry cleaners* and *station*, accompanied by your client's name *Mr Fipps*. See what you have written being absorbed by the balloon, and then reduce it to its original size.

Still mentally holding the string, wrap it around your left ear and relax. Breathe rhythmically for a few moments longer before watching the orange balloon completely disappear.

Experiment with the exercise before using it. You will probably find that it will take time and practise until the technique is fully operational and your mind properly prepared for its use.

Once the balloon method has been fully mastered, the whole week can be programmed in one sitting. When your appointments for the day have been put into the balloon, it must be tied to your ear, then allowed to dissolve completely from your mind.

After each coloured balloon has been filled with the data you wish to remember, touch your forehead with your index and first fingers symbolically to seal the memory. When retrieving memories from the balloons, repeat the same process to enable them to be accessed.

Memory Retrieval

The process of retrieval is quite simple once the programme has been formed in the subconscious mind.

At first, you may find it necessary to find a quiet corner in which to practise. Later, this will not be necessary and your memory balloons will be accessed without following a complicated procedure.

You could be in a position where you need to know your appointments for Friday, but do not have your diary with you. Having mastered the method, it should now take just a split second to locate your schedule. If it is not possible to close your eyes, touch your forehead with your index and first fingers – thus releasing the seal – and mentally locate the appropriate balloon and the colour Indigo. Take a deep breath. Slowly release it, allowing the coloured balloon to remain fixed in the mind. At the same time, mentally request the required information.

If the programme has been established correctly, within moments the balloon will be accessed and the information retrieved. You will find appointments just popping into your mind. It is as simple as that. You would be wrong in thinking that this process of visualisation sounds easier than it is. Once your subconscious mind has been programmed, no effort is needed in accessing the memory balloons. It will work of its own accord.

Having learned to activate your memory processes through visualisation, you will find that your natural memory also improves. In fact, visualisation should be integrated into your training programme. Allow at least ten to fifteen minutes each day for you to practise focusing the attention and visualisation. A lazy memory needs to be approached in an extremely subtle way and the imagery faculty encouraged through visualisation. Developing the imagination is also important when using some of the memory systems covered later.

As well as helping to strengthen the natural memory, visualisation also encourages the improvement of one's powers of observation by precipitating the general awareness. Learning to focus the mind through the imagery faculty that controls the imagination heightens one's awareness in all directions.

You may know the district you live in very well, and can name most of the roads. However, when asked to give a detailed description of the house at the end of the street or say exactly what is beside the church or on the other side of the park, you might come to realise just how little notice you have taken of the area. This is probably so with most people, for we only notice what catches our attention.

However, not only can you improve your memory through visualisation, but it is also quite possible to encourage it to produce memories you did not even realise you knew! A magnificent memory can be cultivated through visualisation to aid the release of the mind's natural powers. Try the following exercise a few times. Make a note of the results. You should be amazed at what you achieve.

An Experience of the Imagination
Sit quietly for a few moments. Follow the usual process of rhythmic breathing until you feel totally relaxed.

Create a mental screen, imagining you are looking down upon the district in which you live.

See the rooftops and chimneys, the roads and the traffic, the park and the church, and people walking. Project yourself totally into the picture. Feel a sense of freedom, almost like a bird able to fly unhindered in any direction you choose. Move into places you have never been before, exploring the entire area rather like a child curiously investigating a new environment.

Move slowly up and down the road in which you live, checking each house and making a mental note of the number on the door. Remind yourself of the names of the people who live there and what they look like. Introduce them into your visualisation experience.

Allow yourself mentally to move behind the houses so you can see the gardens and trees. Let your mind scan the whole environment. Simply follow your curiosity to wherever it wishes to take you.

Be adventurous! Wander away from the area, perhaps to the next district or even an adjacent town. As you take this mental journey you will find pictures coming into your mind of their own accord, almost as though you were watching a film on television. When your mind begins to produce its own images without intervention, you will know that the subconscious mind has been precipitated and memories are beginning to surface.

You may find other events being produced during the visualisation process, such as memories from years gone by. This phenomenon is quite significant when memories have been suppressed, perhaps because of emotional trauma. Accept whatever transpires during your mental journey as an integral part of the memory's natural development. It may take some time for you to familiarise yourself with such mental interaction. But once you have mastered it, you will feel like the pilot at the controls of a helicopter surveying the area known as 'Memory'.

As you move mentally through the district, you will see buildings, road names and other structures you never noticed before. Take a good look at them. Make a mental note of all their details. However, do not allow yourself to be too preoccupied with anything produced during the exercise. At some point, you may feel yourself losing control of the mental journey as the subconscious mind begins to exert its control. Go along with it, but try not to be too analytical. You can terminate the exercise at any point you choose without negative effects.

Second Step

As you allow your mind to transport you, see yourself moving through a mental time barrier into the district as it was when you were a child. Notice how details have changed – the houses, shops, traffic and the way people are dressed. Let your curiosity take you down the street where you lived as a youngster, mentally exploring the whole district where you played. Introduce a childhood friend into the mental journey, letting him or her accompany you. Visit the house where you lived. See how different it was then to the way it is now.

Visit the places you remember going to when you were young, allowing your mind to take you to locations that have long since slipped from your memory. Become totally involved in the mental exercise as though you were physically there.

Go to the park where you played with friends. Pop along to the cinema on the High street. Call in at the local sweet shop. As you do so, feast your eyes on all the different sweets displayed on the counter and along the shelves. Guided completely by your memory, allow yourself to be totally transported into the past.

Very slowly, slip back through the mental time barrier and see the district as it is today. Let your eyes scan the whole area before feeling yourself back in the chair in your home, allowing the picture to fade from your mind.

Sit quietly for a few minutes longer contemplating the experience, then conclude the exercise with rhythmic breathing. Breathe slowly and deeply, allowing your tummy to rise as you breathe in, to fall as you breathe out. Repeat this process a few times before opening your eyes.

Memory Analysis

Make a note of as many details you can recall of your mental journey. On one page of your notebook, enter those with which you were familiar. Meanwhile, on another page list items that did not appear as recognisable.

Look at the scenes that were familiar to you during your visualisation experience and carefully analyse the whole picture. It is also a good idea to confirm what you experienced by physically visiting the places you saw on the mental journey. Once you have ascertained the details your visualisation produced, you should have far more confidence in the exercise.

Practise regularly and the better you will become at controlling the exercise. You should also be more sensitive and aware of details in your surroundings. This is one of the prerequisites of an observant mind. A sharply focused mind is nearly always achieved through visualisation.

Make a separate note of all the details and scenes you could not recognise in your visualisation. Again, check these by physically visiting the places. You will be surprised by the accuracy of the information produced during your mental journey. However, it may take a little practise before positive results are achieved. You might find that this method eventually releases your memory's natural potential, increasing your awareness by one hundred per cent.

There is nothing magical about this exercise. It is designed primarily to encourage and release the memory's natural potential by placing before it various shapes, colours and feelings. Once the memory recognises certain sensations, it responds immediately by producing all the data it has corresponding to them. Visualisation is one of the most effective ways of cultivating the natural memory.

The mind is often likened to a computer whose complexities evade anyone who has not been taught how to use it. However, once instruction is given, the programmes can be accessed and data retrieved. You may encounter a few difficulties with the exercise at the beginning, but with practise the technique will be mastered.

Your mental journey through time is something we all experience when overcome with feelings of nostalgia. This part of the exercise is often productive of emotions that may have been subconsciously suppressed. Try not to terminate the exercise if you find yourself overwhelmed with emotion. Do not avoid it simply because it produces such emotional feelings. As well as aiding the development of the natural memory, an occasional mental sojourn in the past is also good therapy and helps to release suppressed negative thoughts. However, it is not advisable mentally to visit the past too often as this can sometimes produce adverse psychological results.

An efficient memory often develops as a result of an active imagination. Visualisation aids the precipitation of the imagery faculty, creating the bridge between the conscious and the unconscious minds. Further methods will be discussed later on.

9
Remembering Made Easy

Nearly everyone knows just how frustrating it is trying to remember something that did not seem too important when it happened. As a consequence, a weak impression was made upon the mind, resulting in poor recollection. A memory taken for granted is quite often inefficient. But an efficient memory is easily cultivated with exercise and training.

Visualisation will aid your ability to remember immensely. Indeed, quite a few memory techniques rely upon one's ability to visualise and focus the imagination. Most people scan their mental screen in search of the image of whatever they are desperately trying to remember. Without this mental imagery, remembering details becomes that little bit more difficult.

I always encourage visualisation in the development of the natural memory. After all, an artist usually possesses perfect visual recall to enable him or her to convey the correct colours and imagery to the canvas. A writer, too, often relies upon imagination. Visualisation plays an integral part in creating the perfect scenario. Even someone who totally lacks the ability to visualise and create pictures in the mind can be taught the technique.

Try this test. Without taking your eyes from the paper, visualise a door key. See it very clearly on the screen of your mind. Let the image remain for a few moments. Watch the key turn around in your mind. See it from different angles before permitting it to disappear.

Now picture a vase of any colour you choose. As before, very slowly watch it turn around so that you can view it from different angles. Then slowly allow the vase to fade. Remember to keep your eyes open whilst visualising the different objects. You may find this a little more difficult than with your eyes closed, but once you can achieve visualisation with your eyes open, both your powers of concentration and recall will improve immensely.

Next, try to picture a tree, the first tree that comes to mind. See it clearly superimposed over the book in front of you. Again, mentally turn it around, looking at it from different angles. Hold the tree's image for a few moments in your mind before gradually allowing it to vanish.

The object of this visualisation exercise is two-fold. Firstly, it should prove that you are able mentally to recreate images from memory within moments, regardless of whether or not you have any powers of imagination. Secondly, it puts your recall to the test.

Taking the exercise a little further, try and mentally recreate your mother's face, paying particular attention to details such as the nose, eyes, hair and mouth. Make the face truly come alive. Now follow the same procedure and visualise a friend's face. Again, see it clearly in your mind, carefully inspecting the same features. Hold this image for a few moments, then gradually allow it to disappear completely.

Most people are pleasantly surprised at the results. Visual imagery is achieved as a direct result of concentrated thought. In other words, a mental picture is always produced in response to the attention being focused on a specific image or thought.

Very little effort is needed to recreate an object with which you are accustomed. The phenomenon of producing images in the mind's eye is known as Tratak in Yogic terminology. It is experienced during specific methods of meditation, such as the techniques discussed in an earlier chapter.

An efficient memory is dependent upon an actively creative imagination, which can certainly be developed in anyone. Some of the most effective memory systems rely upon visual imagery to support them. At this point, it would be productive to explore various methods and consider how they can work for you.

The Alphabet System

This is a fairly simple technique, and one that requires little effort. It involves using a Key Word that begins with the sound of the letter it represents. For example, A could be represented by any of the following Key Words – APE, ACHE, ACE or AID. When a word has the sound of the letter itself, it should be used as in the key word BEE, to represent the letter B.

The Key Word SEA or even SEE might be employed to denote C, as can SEED or SEEK. As you will have already noticed, the Alphabet System can be learned very quickly, and is far less complicated than the Figure Word Sound System covered in Chapter Three.

Certain words cannot be used because they do not begin with the sound of any of the letters of the alphabet, so would not create an appropriate Key Word image. Some examples are Base, Lace, Dog, Log, Fog, Bottle, Kettle and Ant.

Take a look at the following examples, then try and find your own appropriate Key Words.

A)   APE, ACHE, ACE
B)   BEE, BEAM, BEAD
C)   SEA, SEE, SEAL, SEAM
D)   DEAL, DEEM, DEEP, DEED
E)   EEL, EASE
F)   EFFORT, EFFIGY, EFFICACIOUS
G)   JEEP, JEANS
H)   H-BOMB (No other appropriate key word available)
I)   EYE (Must be the first word) ICON, ICICLE.
J)   JAY (Must be the first choice) JAIL
K)   CANE, CAPE
L)   ELEPHANT, ELOQUENT, ELEMENT, ELABORATE
M)   EMIT, EMULATE, MC
N)   ENSUE, ENTIRE, ENROL
O)   OMEN, OBOE
P)   PEA, PEEL, PEAK
Q)   QUEUE (Must be the first choice) CUPID, CUTE
R)   ARTIST, ARCH
S)   ESTATE, ESKIMO
T)   TEA (Must be the first choice) TEAM, TEAK
U)   YEW
V)   VEAL, VEHICLE
W)   WC (No other appropriate word)
X)   EXTINCT, EXCITE, X-RAY, EXAMPLE
Y)   WIFE, WISE, WHITE
Z)   Z-BEND (No other appropriate word.)

Some of these words may not be acceptable to certain writers on the subject of memory improvement. However, try not to allow this to discourage you from using them if you find that they work for you. Having studied these examples, now try to create your own Key Words by writing next to the appropriate letters:

A)	N)
B)	O)
C)	P)
D)	Q)
E)	R)
F)	S)
G)	T)
H)	U)
I)	V)
J)	W)
K)	X)
L)	Y)
M)	Z)

Now you have completed your own list of Key Words, read through them a few times and try to lodge them firmly in your mind. Next, see if you can recite them from memory, first of all in the correct order, then in reverse. Ask someone to test you by calling letters at random and determine how quickly you are able to recall the Key Word.

Another point to remember is that should you select several Key Words to represent a letter, most memory experts agree it is best to use the one that comes first in the dictionary. This is primarily for ease of recall. If a Key Word ever slips from your mind, simply mentally scan the alphabet until you reach the appropriate letter, thus locating it.

The Alphabet System can be employed by itself or combined with other techniques. You might choose to adapt it to suit your own method of working. In any event, you will find it extremely versatile.

How to Use the Alphabet System
The Alphabet System is also very easy and involves the imagination as much as possible. As long as you understand the images you use

and are able to recall them with ease, this technique will certainly work for you. As the Alphabet System operates in a similar way to the following Figure Image System, the same rules apply.

The Figure Image System

This method is extremely versatile and makes use of figures and images. It necessitates creative imagination. Once fully grasped, it will never be forgotten, especially when you have learned the art of creating personal images.

The Figure Image System employs the numbers one to ten, to which are attached images that resemble the figures. For instance, a finger might represent the number one, though many memory writers use a paintbrush instead. A swan could depict the number two. You might choose to recall the figure three with two mountains or breasts because of the similarity in the shape. Meanwhile, how about a sailing yacht for number four?

It is better and more effective if you create your own images to represent the figures one to ten. To facilitate memory recall, they should ideally be produced from your imagination. However, before you make any attempt, study these examples. Here are the figure images most commonly used:

1	Finger, candle, paintbrush
2	Swan
3	Hills, breasts, heart
4	Yacht
5	Pot-belly, fishing hook
6	Monocle, spoon, pipe
7	Cliff edge, scythe
8	Hour glass, woman's figure, spectacles
9	Head and scarf, a baby sitting, tadpole
10	Bat and ball

These are just to give an idea of what images you should attempt to form. Allow your imagination complete freedom and see what is produced. You may view things in a completely abstract way and be able to use figure images that only seem appropriate and make sense to you. This is acceptable and exactly what the Figure Image

System is about. Nothing else matters as long as it works. Be adventurous. Add or alter it. Create something new to complement it.

Now try and create as many Figure Images as possible, writing them next to the appropriate numbers. As with the other techniques, use your imagination to the maximum. Try to see the images very clearly in your mind's eye. Imagine them as being brightly coloured so they stay in the mind. Make them witty. Do not forget that unusual images facilitate easier and better recall.

1

2

3

4

5

6

7

8

9

10

Memorise your Figure Images. When you feel confident you have lodged them firmly in your mind, close your eyes and recite them, first forwards, then in reverse. Randomly select numbers and see how quickly you can recall the corresponding image. Practise until you can do so without hesitation and you know them off by heart, backwards and forwards. This system will only work effectively when the Figure Images have been perfectly committed to memory and can be recalled quickly and without any effort.

How to use the Figure Image System

The Figure Image System similarly calls for a great deal of creative imagination. Pretend you have a list of ten objects to remember. These are: *A bicycle; a football; a trumpet; a clown's mask; a car tyre; a bottle of Champagne; a fountain pen; a pair of pink boots; a clock; scissors.*

You need to fix these completely different items in your mind so that you can easily recall them. Present them to your memory in the following way, but consider the list very carefully before you decide which Key Images to adopt. As usual, be as imaginative as possible. Use the following examples to give you some idea:

1   Imagine a giant *finger* flicking a huge *football* around a football pitch. Make the imagery hilarious and ridiculous. See the football in bright tones, dressing the finger in the colours of your favourite team. Ensure that the whole picture comes alive sufficiently to impress your memory.

2   Now 'see' a giant *swan* dressed in brightly coloured clothes riding a *bicycle* across the surface of a lake. As before, the sillier the better, for the easier it will be to remember.

3   Mentally picture a man with huge *breasts* and wearing a *clown's mask* dancing joyfully around. Although a fanciful scene, it will help to secure what you need to remember.

4   View yourself lying in the sunshine on the deck of a luxurious *yacht*. You are being serenaded by a beautiful young female playing a *trumpet*.

5   On your mind's mental screen, imagine a huge man with a *pot belly* using a *car tyre* as a hula hoop. See him dancing around the room, looking very foolish

6   Watch a giant *bottle of Champagne* coming alive and wearing a top hat and tails, looking rather curiously at you through a *monocle*. Make the bottle of Champagne extremely animated, almost as though you had stepped into the unreal world of cartoon characters. Again, make everything brightly coloured.

7   For this figure, you may see yourself sitting on the edge of a *cliff top*, holding a giant *fountain pen* and writing your name across the sky. Make the imagery appear unreal. See yourself clearly grasping the giant pen as you sit with your legs hanging over the cliff edge. Yet again, I would suggest being as imaginative as possible, using really bright colours.

8 Pretend you are dreaming of a giant *hourglass* dressed in a policeman's uniform, wearing *pink boots* and trying desperately to be taken seriously. Once more, introduce as many bright colours as you can into the imagery. Do not be afraid in any way to let your creative imagination take the lead.

9 Now see yourself gripping desperately to the big hand of a *clock* suspended from a great height whilst trying to hold a jar of *tadpoles* between your knees. Picture yourself clearly in this ridiculous situation, which is rather like a scene from a silent movie. Ensure that both the clock and the tadpoles feature strongly so that the imagery is firmly implanted. Make the scene very animated as you watch yourself struggling to hold on as though your life depended on it.

10 Imagine two pairs of giant *scissors* playing *bat and ball* at the end of your garden. Be as imaginative as possible as you create this scene of the scissors dancing around, one throwing the ball and the other pair hitting it with the bat.

When using this particular technique, be really adventurous. Only use Key Images that appeal to you and your sense of fun. The object of this method is to create a system of remembering details that works for you, no matter how ridiculous or absurd.

The Box System
They say that moving house is one of the most stressful and traumatic experiences we encounter. Uprooting oneself is difficult enough, but packing can be quite a chore as well as tiring.

Knowing which trunk or tea chest to place belongings in is also very stressful. However, as long as everything is labelled correctly things usually work out in the end. The same can be said of our memories. When they, too, are correctly labelled finding them is less of a problem.

The Box System is probably one of the most simple of memory techniques to learn and use. The principles are very similar to the Cupboard System, which was covered at the beginning of the book.

The first step is to form the programme in the subconscious area of the mind. Find a quiet corner. Sit in a comfortable chair and relax for a few moments. I make no excuse for stressing the importance of slow, rhythmic breathing as this is essential for making the mind peaceful and receptive. It should always be integrated into any mental exercise, such as meditation or visualisation.

With your eyes closed, breathe rhythmically as in previous exercises, making certain that the in-coming breath is mentally sent directly to the brain, and the out-flowing breath takes with it all the toxins that prevent a sharp, clear memory.

When the mind is quiet and the body relaxed, create your mental screen. Focus the attention on it for a few moments. It is important that you are attuned to the programme. When quite relaxed, create in your mind six boxes, each one in a different colour. Use happy, bright hues. It is vitally important to make them come alive.

Express the mental desire to place in the boxes anything and everything you need to remember. See the boxes as externalised compartments of your memory. As you focus your attention on them, know that they may be accessed at any time, in any place. Quietly send a mental affirmation to the subconscious mind enforcing your desire to store memories in the boxes.

Before they can be used, it is vital to spend at least ten minutes each day focusing the attention upon them. Introducing them into your daily visualisation prepares the programme ready for use.

How to Use the Box System

There is nothing complicated whatsoever about the Box System. On the contrary, it is extremely easy to use once the programme has been formed through visualisation. To initiate this technique, simply deposit details to remember in the boxes. But before doing so, the coloured boxes must be categorised in the following way.

Mentally place a number from one to six on each box. The first three are for appointments whilst the remainder deal with miscellaneous matters – in short, anything you need to remember, such as what to buy, jobs to do, birthdays, etc.

As with the Cupboard System, simply place whatever you have to remember in the appropriate box, either whilst in bed or at the end of the day. The following morning, mentally recall the boxes to retrieve whatever is inside. It is vitally important to check your boxes each day. Once you get into the habit of mentally using the boxes, no effort will be needed to make them work for you. Regular visualisation will automatically connect the boxes with your subconscious mind, keeping them alive and active. A little experimentation will help you discover your own method. You may feel that fewer boxes can be used, so the number can be reduced.

The boxes must be mentally recreated every day to keep them alive. This procedure is essential in order to allow the connection with the subconscious mind to be maintained.

Remembering can be made easy with the use of visualisation as it aids the release and cultivation of one's natural memory. In short, visualisation trains the mind and gets it into the habit of producing memories when they are needed.

10
Experimentation and Preparation of the Senses

Keeping the memory active will greatly improve its performance. By presenting it with simple tasks each day, you will help its responses to increase and performance levels to rise. Let us now look at your powers of observation and see how important they are to an efficient memory.

Experiment One
Think of three objects with which you come into contact every day, such as patterned cups, saucers and plates on the dinner table, perhaps the fire surround in your dining room or even the wallpaper pattern. Anything will suffice as long as it is familiar to you on a daily basis.

Without physically studying the selection, close your eyes for a few moments and recreate them one by one in your mind. Try and reconstruct each of the objects in detail. If you are mentally looking at the pattern on the tea service or wallpaper, make a detailed analysis. Ensure the impression is clearly defined, mentally tracing the outline of the intricate pattern as far as you can recall it.

Follow the same procedure with whatever you have chosen mentally to recreate. Recollect all the details of shape, pattern, texture and even temperature. Spend some time on each feature and characteristic until you are totally certain that the analysis you have made is accurate. The exercise may be concluded when you are satisfied that you have recalled as much information about the objects as possible.

For the second part of the experiment, you should now physically look at your chosen items to see just how much detail you missed. Spend at least five minutes making a thorough study, taking care to examine all their features. Now that you know the point of the exercise is mentally to photograph all the details, you should be more meticulous with your analysis so that a clearer impression is fixed in the memory.

When you are confident you have acquired enough information to recall the objects in full, make yourself a cup of tea just to take your mind completely away from the experiment for half an hour or so.

Once the mind is refreshed, sit quietly with your eyes closed, and follow the same procedure. First of all, allow each object quickly to pass through your mind one by one. Next, very slowly recall the first item to the mental screen. See its shape. Make it appear almost solid in your mind. Slowly and meticulously begin your analysis of the details. Now see how much information you are able to recall. Spend time with each object until you have fully exhausted all the information you have in your memory bank.

Unless we are told to do so beforehand, we pay very little attention to detail. Just a little training in observation helps us to be far more receptive to the impulses of the external world, aiding the cultivation of a good memory.

Being observant not only suggests the ability to notice detail: audible observation must also be considered in the descriptive analysis. Allowing all the senses to be totally involved is extremely important when observing anything. We exercise our senses all the time by seeing, hearing, touching, tasting and smelling. Should one of these be defective, the knowledge we have of what is around us would be incomplete.

When you are involved in conversation or perhaps listening to a lecture at university, to allow your attention to wander even for a split second would probably cause you to lose the thrust of what is being said and could throw everything completely out of context. It is therefore important to cultivate the habit of paying attention to what is said, even if it means closing your eyes to eliminate all other distractions.

Our sense of hearing plays an extremely important part in the accumulation and simulation of information. When a Native American Indian youth became a man, he was blindfolded, taken into a forest, and forced to sit quietly until the sun went down. This was done in order that he would pay total attention to the sounds of nature. He had to listen carefully and to make a mental note of every sound that came to his ears so he would learn to recognise in an instant the sounds from different creatures. Focusing the attention on a specific faculty precipitates its development, making it more sensitive to its appropriate vibrations.

Experiment Two

Take yourself into the garden or go to an open window. Sit quietly with your eyes closed. Relax for a few minutes to allow yourself to become accustomed to the sound of your breathing and to attune your thoughts to the surrounding environment.

When you feel quite comfortable and your mind is quiet, listen to the external sounds collectively manifesting in the small space of your eardrum. Gradually go through the process of mentally isolating each individual sound and becoming aware of its source. Allow your awareness to home in on each sound, carefully registering it mentally – birds singing; dogs barking; people talking; car horns; traffic; children playing; leaves rustling on trees. See exactly how many different sounds you can hear in the air around you.

When you have done this, allow your range of hearing to transcend the immediate noises. Let it extend beyond the sounds until you become almost oblivious to all external noise. Become attuned to those sounds that are almost inaudible to the physical ear. For a few moments experience complete stillness of thought and breath. Permit this state to continue for a few minutes longer, then relax.

To some this may seem a pretty pointless exercise, but for the long-term development of the memory it is extremely effective. It needs to be practised regularly and allowed to become an integral part of your memory training programme. When the exercise has been concluded, a record should be kept of everything you heard and experienced.

The same procedure can be followed with visual observation of everything around you. With this practice, you should physically eliminate all external sound by either plugging the ears with cotton wool or simply limiting your hearing by covering them.

With the visual exercise, you need to make a mental note of all your surroundings – the look of the sky, the way in which clouds collectively form. Become totally aware of the colours and shades of everything around you. Notice the movement and rhythm of the trees and the grass. Pay particular attention to shape and colour. Try to imagine the texture of everything you see. Allow yourself mentally to merge with everything before your eyes. Do not simply look: mentally absorb as though you were taking a photograph with your mind.

When you feel ready, slowly conclude the exercise and relax for a few minutes. Keeping a record of your feelings and making a note of everything you saw is vitally important to this particular exercise. You will be surprised at how many things you noticed.

Although the same procedure should be followed fairly regularly, it would be unwise to force yourself to practise this exercise. This would merely defeat the purpose, which is purely to develop the senses. A bored or disinterested mind is not an observant one.

Absent-mindedness
Whether because of tiredness or lack of concentration, most people experience absent-mindedness at some time. A common example is when you mislay the car keys and are late for an appointment. We all know just how maddening it is when the memory will simply not work.

When next you find yourself in this or a similar predicament, you must access your subconscious mind for help. Subconsciousing is the process of calling upon the memory to reveal what you have forgotten.

Subconsciousing
When you try in vain to remember where you put your car keys the subconscious action of Association is often effective in aiding the process of recall.

Sit quietly with your eyes closed. Mentally retrace your steps to the place where you remember last having your keys. Recreating the episode in your mind – and silently expressing the need to find them – will cause one situation mentally to bring forth another. You may have to repeat this process a few times before the memory of where you left the keys finally pops into your mind.

Similarly, if you have forgotten something extremely important someone has told you to do – perhaps at work – again sit quietly for a few moments and think of the nearest conversation that preceded it. Usually, the reproduction of one component will produce in the mind impressions created by another until finally the memory produces what it is you are trying to remember.

In the process of preparing the senses, making the mind more receptive and the memory more efficient, the overall mental performance must be considered. A serious intention to train the mind necessitates persistence of attention: someone who lacks attention and is not mentally persistent with anything often possesses a weak memory. In this case, I would suggest that a more systematic approach to cultivating the senses be adopted, using a programme that is designed to suit your requirements and capabilities. Taking one stage at a time is important, presenting the mind with a series of easy tasks to exercise it.

For instance, everyone can recite the alphabet, but difficulties arise when asked to do so in reverse order. Study the alphabet for a few moments, then attempt to say it backwards from memory.

A B C D E F G H I J K L M N O
P Q R S T U V W X Y Z

Unless you have previously learned it in reverse, it is unlikely you were successful with the first attempt. However, when you apply a little strategy and organise the letters in a way that the mind will comprehend, saying the alphabet backwards becomes less of a problem. I would suggest breaking it into groups, as we did with figures earlier on.

ZYX WVU TSR QPO NML KJI HGF EDC BA

Study the letters for a few moments, then try to commit them to memory. You should now find it a lot easier to memorise.

Training the memory to be efficient is one task, but teaching it to remember quickly is another. Once you have discovered your own special method of recalling different facts from the memory bank, you should concentrate on your speed of remembering.

In an earlier chapter, we explored the concept of Catenation, or linking details together. When the mind is presented with two completely unrelated words, to memorise them it helps to interject another word that may be associated with either of the two unconnected words. This will unite them so they are placed firmly in the memory. This method of association is very easy, yet extremely effective.

Although we previously explored Catenation, see how quickly you can think of appropriate words to unify the following extremes. Spend no more than five minutes studying the list, then notice how you do with your first attempt. Repeat the exercise a few times before looking at my list.

1	DOG	WIFE
2	LETTER	ACHE
3	BLOOD	BALANCE
4	LETTER	SQUAD
5	FIRE	CHAIR
6	LIGHT	BOAT
7	ARM	LIFT
8	PLANT	PURCHASE
9	DOOR	GAME
10	ROAD	FORWARD
11	CLAY	DOWN
12	CLOTHES	DRAWN
13	GARDEN	HOUSE
14	FLOWER	SETTEE
15	BROAD	FISH
16	DEEP	FILTER
17	SHOE	SCARF
18	HOUR	DOOR
19	HALF	OUT
20	PAPER	GANG

Now here is my list:

1) Fish 2) Head 3) Bank 4) Bomb 5) Arm 6) House 7) Chair 8) Hire 9) Panel 10) Way 11) Pipe 12) Horse 13) Gate 14) Bed 15) Sword 16) Water 17) Lace 18) Glass 19) Way 20) Chain

Having performed this exercise a few times, repeat it just once more, but avoid using the same words and see what you devise. Also remember to check how long it takes to accomplish.

This is not so much a test for your memory as it is for your ability to think quickly. The more you repeat something, the stronger the impression it makes upon your memory and the quicker you are able to recall it.

When presented with a series of letters and figures that appear in a recognisable sequence, we have no problem reciting them from memory. However, if the sequence is altered slightly we need to apply a little more effort. Look at the following list for a few moments. You will immediately recognise the order and be able to recite it from memory.

A1. B2. C3. D4. E5. F6. G7. H8. I9. J10. K11. L12. M13. N14. O15. P16. Q17. R18. S19. T20. U21. V22. W23. X24. Y25. Z26.

When the figure sequence is amended just a little, more effort is needed to remember it. Now study this list:

A2. B3. C4. D5. E6. F7. G8. H9. I10. J11. K12. L13. M14. N15. O16. P17. Q18. R19. S20. T21. U22. V23. W24. X25. Y26. Z27.

However, as soon as you figure out the changes, the code is quickly learned. Commit the last sequence to memory and see how rapidly you can recite it. The speed of your ability to learn the second sequence will tell you how quick are your responses. If you encountered no problems with the second sequence, at this point your memory should show signs of efficiency improvement.

I still maintain that artificial aids are no substitute for a good natural memory. Some techniques in this book will certainly aid the development of the natural memory and also help the development of all the senses. As stressed, the memory needs to be encouraged and presented with the correct methods. Once the memory processes have been precipitated, you will be able to access the subconscious areas of the mind with very little effort and remember any details with greater ease.

Most people are only able to remember items when they are given in a specific order or sequence. If it is altered in any way their ability to recall is impaired. Bearing this in mind, to make the memory more capable matters must be presented in the ordered sequence it understands.

Take poetry. The rhyme and rhythm allow one word to give forth another. Prose is more difficult to commit to memory because its rhythm is inconsistent and there is no rhyme to follow.

Developing a Dynamic Memory

Most memory experts agree about one aspect – that within the mind there is great potential. We all have the ability to release its immense power and to develop a dynamic memory. Using simple methods, you can access your memory banks as easily as though you were flicking through the pages of an encyclopaedia.

A focused and yet systematic approach is all that is needed for the cultivation of consistent memory release. The majority of people take their memories for granted and therefore put very little effort into the process of remembering.

To improve the efficiency of our memory we need to give the information we place in it some semblance of order. To achieve this, we can create Memory Pegs or Hooks upon which to hang memories so that we know exactly where to find them when needed.

Imagine several hangers in the wardrobe upon which your coats are placed. No matter how long you leave them there, when you return they will all still be there. The same applies to memories. Once memory pegs have been created and your memories are firmly affixed, you will be able to recall them with great ease.

Information that has been properly learned and lodged solidly in the mind becomes knowledge – and knowledge cannot be forgotten. You may disagree and say, 'That's ridiculous! Most of the information I acquired through my studies at college has gone from my mind. It is nearly all completely forgotten.' My response must be that knowledge is never forgotten, only misplaced.

Primarily due to lack of use, we may forget into which memory compartment we have placed information. But its retrieval is often spontaneously produced by an associated idea that serves as a memory peg, facilitating recall. So knowledge cannot be forgotten, no matter how hard you try.

Your name is a prime example. Think of yourself for a few moments. Say your name and mentally see it written in front of you. Now allow it to disappear and try to forget it completely. You cannot. It is impossible to forget your name because you know it, and it is knowledge.

Now we have established this fact, let us explore the concept of a Dynamic Memory and take a look at how this can be achieved.

Memory Test One
Read through the following, then see how much you can remember by repeating it into a cassette recorder.

Having done so, take your mind away and enjoy a cup of tea. After the break, go through the story again and follow the same procedure. You should be surprised at how much detail you managed to recall this time, and just how quickly and easily you were able to remember the story.

Do so twice more. Each time, increase the speed of reading so it is quicker than previous attempts. Remember to repeat the story from memory when you finish reading it. Recording what you read will help your speed and efficiency of recall.

It is also essential to see in your mind what you are reading. Picture it clearly. Make it come alive as though you were physically present. As with earlier exercises, use bright and vivid colours, ensuring that the characters are animated. Project yourself into the situation as you read it. Feel a part of the events, experiencing the humour and delight of everything you witness.

Sit quietly for a few moments before reading through the following situation. Begin to read when your mind is quiet.

Imagine the Eiffel Tower silhouetted against a clear Spring sky. Make it appear solid and substantial, clearly defined against the Paris background. Hanging on the side of the Eiffel Tower you can see a dancing chimpanzee. In its right hand it is holding a copy of your favourite newspaper, and in its left hand a bag of glowing orange butterflies.

The chimpanzee empties the bag of butterflies, which float down to settle on the roof of a pink taxi. Driving the pink taxi is Michael Jackson. Sitting beside him is an Old English Sheepdog called Harry.

The Old English Sheepdog is wearing a bright green suit and sun-glasses, and is sipping Pepsi from a long glass. The sheepdog catches sight of a black cat crossing the busy road. He barks excitedly as he jumps from the taxi to give chase, spilling his Pepsi across Michael Jackson, causing the taxi to knock over the Eiffel Tower. Harry, the Old English Sheepdog, climbs back into the taxi covered in glowing orange butterflies, accompanied by the smiling black cat.

Before you begin repeating it into a cassette recorder, pause for a few moments, allowing the story to pass quickly through your mind, frame by frame, without any dialogue. Repeat this process twice, and then speak into the recorder.

After the third reading, you will notice how the whole story somehow presents itself in your mind, almost in one instant flash. The situation contains several memory pegs that aid image processing and immediate recall. The technique assists the development of a dynamic memory and the cultivation of long-term memory retrieval.

I appreciate that the made-up story about Michael Jackson and the other characters would never really occur, but you will shortly see exactly why such a ridiculous situation is used.

Follow the instructions – and notice just how easily the account can be recalled. As suggested, read it through four times, increasing the speed on each occasion. Follow the same procedure when repeating it from memory. Again, see how quickly it has taken you to memorise the entire story.

Unless there is something drastically wrong with your brain, as well as your name there are many other facts that are impossible to forget. These are details you have learned well and truly, and are programmed into your memory. Each object with which you come into contact in daily life is now knowledge and therefore firmly rooted in the memory. Let me repeat that you cannot forget knowledge.

Memory Test Two

Before reading through this exercise, sit comfortably for a few moments to prepare the mind. Mentally picture a room in your house, preferably not the one in which you are sitting. Mentally see the room completely empty, then think how you would like to see it furnished.

Begin by placing the following items around the room: 1) An armchair in the corner by the window. 2) A table under the window. 3) Bookshelves against the wall to your right. 4) A stool by the bookshelves. 5) A settee in front of the table. 6) A standard lamp. 7) A writing bureau. Mentally rearrange the room to your liking, then deposit each article in your mind.

1 – Armchair
2 – Table
3 – Bookshelves
4 – Stool
5 – Settee
6 – Standard lamp
7 – Writing bureau

Step One

Now you have the room furnished the way you want, study the list of items, and try to secure them in your mind in the order they appear.

Close the book. Begin reciting the list in order of sequence beginning with One –Armchair, Two – Table, Three – Bookshelves, etc.

Repeat the list aloud several times, always saying the number of sequence first. When you are confident that you have implanted the items firmly in your memory, deliver them in reverse order.

Step Two

Pause for a few moments, then repeat the same procedure, beginning with the correct order. As you say each article, see it very clearly in your mind. The imagery should be precise as though seeing it solidly in the room before you.

As you mentally repeat the list again, take time with each object and allow it to be visually created in your mind. Pause between each piece of furniture. Do not move to the following one until you have a clear and vivid image of each item in your mind.

Step Three

When you have completed the list of furniture, move back to the beginning and increase your speed. Say the word and visualise the object. See its colour and shape. Make it solid as if you could reach out and touch it, or even sit on it.

Repeat the process over and over. Increase your speed and improve the imagery more each time. Do not pause for any reason whatsoever until you are completely satisfied with the results.

Step Four

When you are certain that the imagery of each object is clear and embedded firmly in your memory, repeat the process in reverse. Again, see the piece of furniture clearly in your mind whilst saying the word out aloud.

View the images quickly passing through your mind as you simultaneously announce what they are. Repeat the procedure until you are confident that they are firmly lodged in the memory.

Step Five

Unless the images are visualised vividly in your mind's eye, the point of the exercise will be defeated completely. Now you should visualise the pieces of furniture passing rapidly through your mind almost in one instant.

Resist the temptation to speak or even think what they are. Just allow them to pass through your consciousness at an incredibly fast speed. Repeat this process backwards and forwards a few times before resting.

At first, you may encounter difficulty visualising the pieces of furniture passing this rapidly through the mind. Should this be the case, allow the process to be as fast as possible, gradually increasing speed until you reach maximum rapidity.

Remember to avoid writing down details as this merely makes the memory sluggish and lazy, and defeats the object of the programme altogether.

The primary aim of the furniture exercise is to increase the memory's responses and to show just how quickly you can recall details. Practise over and over again until the objects flow almost of their own accord through your mind.

Do not move to the next chapter until you are certain that you have achieved rapid thinking. Once mastered, this ability will enable you to use the following system effectively. You can rest assured that by the end of the book you will have the means to develop a Dynamic Memory. This will take minimum effort and just a little time each day.

12
Rapid Thinking and Memory Pegs

A memory peg is simply a place to store memories so that you know exactly where they are. It can be likened to a toolbox in which you put tools to locate the one you want immediately. The process of creating Memory Pegs – or Hooks as they are sometimes called – is very easy. These are words lodged solidly in the mind and which you can never forget.

In Chapter Eleven, I asked you to fix seven pieces of furniture in your memory and recite them backwards and forwards as quickly as possible. Once cemented in the memory, the seven items of furniture become Memory Pegs and may be used as such to aid you in the process of remembering other details. The names of these everyday items of furniture can never be forgotten as they are programmed into your mind as knowledge.

The only aspect you have to learn in the process of fixing Memory Pegs firmly in the mind is the order or sequence in which you place them in the memory. Once this has been successfully achieved, you will have a reliable mental Filofax, and possess the ability to recall long lists of objects.

A dynamic memory is meticulously tidy and well organised, and able instantly to locate information and recall it from the memory bank. Let us now explore the use of Memory Pegs and the concept of a Dynamic Memory.

Other details that are often used as Memory Pegs and which can never be forgotten are parts of our body. If you are still a little sceptical about the whole subject, you will probably find this a ridiculous notion. But look at it logically: we are inseparable from our bodies – and to forget them is impossible. It makes sense to use what we know well as a Memory Peg. Our body and its individual components fit that category perfectly.

You have already previously experienced the rapidity with which you can visualise objects, and hopefully now possess a fairly good idea exactly how that ability can aid you in the cultivation of a capable memory.

Step Six
For this exercise you will need to stand. With your eyes open, mentally scan your body from your feet to your head. Select ten parts to use as Memory Pegs. Read through this list five or six times, and touch the part of the body that corresponds with each word. As you do so, try to secure it in the mind.

1 – TOES
2 – KNEES
3 – HIPS
4 – TUMMY
5 – CHEST
6 – SHOULDER
7 – NECK
8 – NOSE
9 – FOREHEAD
10 – CROWN OF HEAD

Read through the list once more, trying to visualise the part of your body that corresponds with the word without touching it. Allow the images to be vivid and come alive in your mind. See them as being solid and substantial. If you have difficulty in visualising, put as much effort as you can into imagining them. However you achieve the experience, feel as though you can physically see all the parts of your body as the words pass slowly through your mind.

Step Seven
Study the list of body parts for another five minutes or so and try to strengthen their image in your mind. Do so in the correct order, then in reverse.

When you are quite certain you have memorised all ten body parts, begin reciting them out loud from memory, always calling the number first.

Move through the list fairly quickly in the correct order from one to ten, then in reverse.

Repeat this several times or more until a reasonable speed has been achieved. When you are completely satisfied that all ten body parts have been secured firmly in the memory, try to increase your speed.

Do not permit your concentration to wander even for a split second, as this will cause the rhythm to be interrupted. Maintain the rhythm and speed for a little while longer, then have a rest.

It is of paramount importance to the exercise that you visualise the words as they pass rapidly through your mind and maintain the speed as they do so.

Now try repeating the list one more time backwards and forwards, but this time increasing the speed to its maximum. See the corresponding images passing quickly through your mind with such rapidity that you almost have no control over them.

Repeat this process for as long as you possibly can, then take a break.

Step Eight

You should now repeat the exercise, only this time it is not necessary to say the words. Simply allow the images that correspond with them to pass rapidly through your mind. Watch them in silence without allowing your mind to produce the words. Again, repeat the process backwards and forwards several times before pausing for a rest.

You should now have an excellent Memory Peg system with which to work. Let us now place some items that we need to remember in the Memory Pegs:

1) Watermelon 2) Lampshade 3) Onions 4) Tin of paint
5) Fresh cream 6) Curtains 7) Houseplant 8) Bunch of roses
9) Packet of balloons 10) Candles

The Memory Pegs are now fixed solidly in your mind so cannot be forgotten. The fact that they are parts of your body make them even stronger and more difficult to forget. Anything else you attach to the pegs will also be lodged in the memory.

You need now to attach the details you must remember to your Memory Pegs. Before you go through the process of pegging, you must understand the fundamental principles underlying the procedure. It is no use whatsoever simply attaching the articles to be remembered to the Memory Pegs: this is simply not good enough. They must be secured to the pegs with humorous or ridiculous imagery. Make it completely illogical or perhaps create something that could not possibly happen in reality, rather like a scene from one of your favourite cartoons.

Although you already have your Memory Pegs in place, a ridiculous situation created around what you need to remember acts like a mental adhesive.

For instance, your first Memory Peg is *toes*, to which you could attach the *melon*. By itself, a melon would not catch the imagination and be boring. To make it more interesting so it is fixed firmly in the memory, you must evolve a silly happening. Visualise the melon with a face, arms and legs, dancing around your feet. Make it as animated as possible.

Imagine yourself kicking the melon. See it holding on tightly to your toes. Nothing could be funnier or more ridiculous. That is all you need to do to be able to recall the melon: it is now fixed in your memory. When you are shopping and cannot remember what you have to buy, just go quickly through your Memory Pegs until you arrive at the appropriate one – and you can be certain that your toes will cause the melon to spring out of your memory.

The second item on the shopping list – *lampshade* –could be attached to your second Memory Peg, *knees*. Have fun visualising the lampshade. Perhaps visualise your knees with smiling faces, wearing lampshades for hats, and singing happily.

The third article is *onions*. You might imagine two giant onions hanging from your third Memory Peg, *hips*. Because they are so heavy, see them weighing you down, causing you to sink into the ground. I cannot stress too much the importance of making the imagery as real and as animated as possible.

The fourth object on your list, *tin of paint*, can be linked to the corresponding Memory Peg, *tummy*. Possibly, you could imagine paint spilling all over your tummy. See yourself looking down in horror.

Imagine a huge tub of *fresh cream* being poured all over your *chest* – the fifth Memory Peg. Picture yourself trying desperately to lick it off. Make it as absurd as you can, full of animation and bright colours. You may like to add something or perhaps change it completely.

The sixth article is *curtains*. You could imagine a multi-coloured pair with a life of their own, moving slowly around your *shoulder*, the sixth Memory Peg. See the curtains draped across your shoulders, brightly coloured and alive. This visualisation has a lot of possibilities.

Now turn to the next item on your list, *houseplant*. Imagine one growing out the side of your *neck*, the seventh Memory Peg. Once more, be as imaginative as you possibly can to make it more concrete in the mind.

Next, see a *bunch of roses* blooming out of your *nose*, the eighth Memory Peg. Watch yourself pulling them out, but the harder you tug, the bigger they grow. Make the roses different colours. Let there be a lot of action in the imagery. Allow your imagination to run wild.

Balloons – the ninth article on your shopping list – can be visualised attached to your *forehead*, pulling you into the air. See yourself struggling to stay on the ground, but the different coloured balloons just float off, taking you with them.

Lastly, imagine huge *candles* sticking out of the *crown of your head*, the tenth Memory Peg. Visualise the candles dripping wax all over your head. I cannot stress too much the importance of liveliness and colour. Again, make the imagery as ridiculous as possible to help secure it in your memory.

There is nothing complicated about using Memory Pegs. Once established in the subconscious, the memory will always produce whatever you have pegged to it.

No effort will be needed when you have created your Memory Pegs and planted them firmly in your mind. The eventual release of the memory's full potential also comes about as a direct consequence. By the end of this book, you will be surprised with the rapidity of your memory recall, and the way it has become finely attuned.

Earlier, we used items of furniture upon which to focus the memory and to produce a more rapid response to recall. The increased rapidity of thought you experienced in that exercise hopefully will have helped in preparing your mind for the method we are now going to explore.

Now that you know exactly how to use the peg technique, we will take a look at the Room System and the use of furniture as Memory Pegs.

The Room System

As usual, sit quietly for a few moments, and then mentally create a plan of a house. See four rooms. Look at them one by one, noticing how the furniture is positioned.

Mentally empty all the rooms and visualise each room in turn without furniture.

Carefully select five articles of furniture you wish to put in each room, placing each piece exactly as you want. Give careful consideration to the positioning of the furniture. The imagery in your visualisation should appear vivid and real. Become totally involved in it.

When your rooms are completely furnished, number each article of furniture from one to twenty. Once this is done, allow your mind to move from room to room, slowly looking at each number, beginning with one and concluding with twenty. At the beginning, it may be a good idea if you make a list of the furniture to help you to fix it in the memory.

Programming the Memory Pegs

As with the previous exercise, call out all the items of furniture from one to twenty, beginning each time with the number. For example, number one – chair, number two – couch, and so on. Move from room to room, and from one piece of furniture to another. On reaching number twenty, repeat the process. Recite the furniture in the correct order, then in reverse.

You will probably encounter little difficulty in memorising the articles of furniture. The problem is usually embedding the sequential order in the memory. Once this is done, your Furniture Peg System will be programmed and ready to use.

Name the pieces of furniture forwards and backwards until you feel confident that your recitation is initiated almost without thinking and with great ease. Take a short break, then repeat the process, gradually increasing the speed, again forwards and backwards.

Once you have reached your maximum speed, visualise the furniture passing quickly through your mind in silence. Watch it move at an incredible speed, almost out of your control. Now take a rest.

When all the pieces of furniture have been rooted in your memory and you can recite them quickly both ways, you are ready to begin the process of pegging.

Pegging

You can use furniture in exactly the same way as body pegs. Simply link the details you need to recall to your furniture: it is as simple as that. Should you have to remember to buy a cardigan, attach it to a piece of furniture and create humorous imagery around it.

Imagine, perhaps, that you can see an animated armchair with a face, arms and legs, draped in a large, brightly coloured *cardigan*. As with previous exercises, ensure it is as lively and amusing as possible to fix firmly in the memory.

Your furniture pegs are fixed in the memory bank so cannot be forgotten. Anything you attach to these memory pegs will also be impossible to forget, and recalled with great ease.

Simply continue the same process of linking to each article of furniture all the items from the list you need to remember. When you wish to recall them, simply go through your twenty pieces of furniture until the appropriate one is reached, and the object you require will literally spring to mind. That is all there is to it.

Of course, the peg system may be used to store long lists of unrelated details. Once created, you have formed an excellent filing system that will never let you down.

It is essential to exercise your mind as much as possible by setting yourself a daily training schedule. Combined with simple exercises, visualisation is important to keep the mind supple. Use the techniques whenever you can to enable them to be programmed into your memory system.

Exercises involving concentration are also vitally important in the cultivation of the memory. Learning to focus the attention greatly improves the powers of observation, cementing what is stored in the memory bank.

13

More Ideas for Remembering Names

If something does not impress your mind strongly enough to lodge it in the memory, you have to create a ploy that will cause it to do so. It matters little how you achieve this as long as it helps in the process of recall.

In Chapter Five, I covered techniques for remembering faces, and explained the importance of paying attention to someone's name when it is given. The following method requires noticing the detail of the face. This is used primarily to remember names by using another word that sounds similar to the name, combined with a mental picture. Although the sound of the word is the most important, visual imagery helps with the recall.

When going through the process of fixing *Bill* in the memory, you need to find a name that sounds similar. Bill is quite easy, and also produces a strong picture. You could use the bill of a duck, which would give you an extremely animated image of a duck quacking. Perhaps you would prefer to use bill as in electricity bill. Although the latter would produce a fairly definite image, a duck is far more effective.

The sound does not have to be exactly that of the name. Some are quite hard and bear no resemblance to anything else whatsoever, so you would have to use the nearest sound. *Chris* might be a little difficult, so crisp would suffice. The visual image and the sound of the word give you the name. You could imagine a giant crisp and see yourself nibbling it.

For *Tom*, you might use tom-toms, as in small drums. Tom-toms create a good, clear image with the cartoon character of your choice beating them. *Tomato* could also be employed to represent *Tom*. Tomato would be an amusing image. See a giant tomato man dancing in front of you. Using the word tomato would immediately cause Tom to spring into your mind. Meanwhile, the American 'John', as in 'toilet', could represent the name John, creating some hilarious imagery.

It is also useful if the person to whom the name belongs has some obvious or unusual features or characteristics, such as a large nose, big ears or even a fat, red face. Always take notice of the individual to whom you are introduced. Listen carefully to the name. Remembering someone's name is possibly the best compliment you can pay them. In the world of commerce, this is extremely important and represents a conscientious, interested business person.

Study this list and find words that you think sound similar. Make a note of them on a separate piece of paper.

ALLAN	CATHY	EMMA
ADAM	DONALD	FRED
ANDREW	DICK	FLO
ANTHEA	DEBBIE	PHIL
AUDREY	DONNA	PETER
BETTY	DEREK	PAT
BEN	DESMOND	PAUL
COLIN	ETHEL	ROSE
CONNIE	EDDIE	ROB
SIMON	VIOLET	BEVERLY
SID	VIC	CHRIS
SAM	VAL	TOM
STAN	VINNY	JOHN
TOM	WILLY	JACK
TERRY	WALTER	JANE
TANIA	WENDY	JADE
UNA	YVONNE	JILL
KATE	GERRY	HARRY
BRIDGET	GABBY	HENRY
IAN	ISOBEL	ALBERT
LYN	LEN	LIBBY
CARL	CANDY	PEGGY
NELLIE	STELLA	HELEN

Use your imagination as much as possible. This system will never allow you to forget a face, and also helps to remember up to a hundred names, sometimes more. The concept is primarily finding words that sound like the name itself. Names are mostly abstractions so often hard to recall.

However, some immediately suggest a word with a strong visual picture, such as *Penny*. Two images spring to mind, a *pen* and a *knee,* so could be combined. You might imagine a huge pen sitting across your knee. Some names give an immediate visual image and require very little effort to imagine.

Although abstractions, certain names are similar to other words, such as *Burt* or *Bert*. This sounds like *burnt* so one could employ it. The imagination will provide all sorts of images – burning wood, burning food on a cooker, even burnt food on a plate.

Debbie sounds remarkably like *dead bee* whereas *Tony* automatically creates a picture of a *toe* and a *knee*. You might see something completely different. Use it as long as it comes from your imagination and the image immediately helps you to recall the name.

Pauline might suggest *leaning pole*, and *Grace* indicate *prayer* or *grass*. Remember to go with exactly what the sound of the name suggests to you. Even if the image you form sounds ridiculous and means nothing to other people, as longs as it helps you to recall the name that is all that matters.

It is always best to use the first image the name suggests. It might not sound at all like the name, but as long as you can hear the name in it and are able to create an effective visual image, it will help your recollection.

Names like *Morris* or *Maurice* might suggest *more rice*, or you could hear something completely different. Once you have fully grasped the concept of creating visual images and sounds to help you recall names, you will immediately be able to create the appropriate imagery. It takes only a little practise, but is extremely effective.

Other Useful Methods for Remembering Names

Children often couple a name with another word, that perhaps rhymes – *Sid the lid; John the scone; Joan the bone; Len the pen; Terry the berry; Ann the can; Tom the bomb; Jean the bean*. The list is endless and open to literally thousands of possibilities. This may seem silly, but as long as works it does not matter.

The word you use with the name can perhaps suggest some characteristic or feature. *Ted* has a large head, so you could remember him by creating the imagery of *Ted the head*. William might appear stupid so you might employ visual imagery around *Willie is silly*.

If Clifford appears to smell rather strongly, there are two obvious choices – *Cliff the niff* or *Cliff the sniff*. Terry may always be smiling, which leads to *Terry is merry*. Meanwhile, Carol is a little over weight. *Carol the barrel* would help you to remember her.

Mathew seems a little eccentric, hence *Matty is batty*, whereas Jane is quite plain, leading to *Plain Jane*.

Even when someone has no obvious feature or characteristic that would suggest a word to rhyme with their name, any rhyming word will suffice. *Kate the gate* produces strong imagery to help you to recall her whilst *Lynn the pin* suggests this name, even more so if the young woman is slenderly built.

June the balloon again produces strong visual imagery, especially if she is quite plump. You could see her attached to a large balloon, floating into the sky.

Douglas can be remembered by shortening the name and using *Doug the bug*. Imagining a giant bug would help immediately. Then there is Wayne and *Wayne the train*. His name will be easily recalled just by visualising a train.

You would be forgiven for thinking this method is somewhat juvenile. But once you have programmed the technique into your mind and fully grasped it, recalling names will be as simple as the system suggests.

As with similar methods, allow your imagination total freedom. Always create vivid imagery attached to the rhyme. It may seem a little too easy to be true, but you will find it extremely effective once you get the hang of it. Try it for yourself with these examples:

Loll; Betty; Hugh; Steve; Jason; Peggy; Danny; Dave; Mark; Bob; June; Donna; Ethel; Barbara; Graham; Gary; Jan; Fran; Paul; Ian; Sally; Milly; Ryan; Jenny; Carl; Jack; Lucy; Rose; Mick; Alf; Sandy.

Showing interest in everyone you meet whether or not they are important can only be good for you in the workplace. Always listen very attentively when a name is given. It really does not pay to be selective when your work involves meeting people. You must cultivate the habit of paying *attention* and being *observant* if you are ever to be successful and further your career.

Although slightly more difficult, surnames can also be treated in exactly the same way as first names. At school I was sometimes called *Roberts the robot*. There was also an extremely overweight young lad whose surname was *Cale*. Other children used to call him *Cale the whale*. Although cruel, it brought his name to mind with great ease.

Should this technique for remembering appeal to you, list all the names of which you can think. Study them. Write down visual rhymes to help recall them. Take time with each name. Come up with as many ideas as you can for each one.

This method of rhyme will also aid the cultivation of a sharper natural memory. It is also an ideal tool to assist intuition, extremely useful when your work involves meeting and dealing with different people.

The Art of Remembering a Conversation

When introduced to someone, I like him or her to look at me, not over my shoulder. Apart from being good manners, it also shows you are taking an interest in the meeting.

Allowing your eyes to wander during a conversation shows complete disregard for the person to whom you are speaking. Even when the topic of conversation fails to stimulate and hold your interest, it is polite to look as though you are following it carefully.

However, should your work involve meeting lots of people, the onus is certainly on you to pay careful attention to what is said either to you or someone else in the company. Always be attentive, for this will develop your senses. Listening to exactly what is said and watching what is taking place brings about the individual development and integration of the auditory and visual responses.

Eye contact is an essential part of one-to-one conversation as this allows the listener to take control of the interactive process. Watching the person's facial expressions and eye movement whilst simultaneously listening to what is being said causes the substance of the conversation to be rooted firmly in the memory.

Very little effort is needed to quickly get the basis of a conversation. As long as the main points of what is being said are lodged in the mind, these will automatically suggest the rest of the conversation when it is needed.

This technique may also be used when trying to listen to two conversations at the same time. Training the sense of hearing to do so simultaneously is not as silly or impossible as it sounds. Using peripheral hearing is an ability many people possess without realising it. I am certain you have been in the situation where two people were trying to get their points of view over at the same time, so you found yourself being forced to listen to both of them.

You probably got the gist of what was being said, even though you were unable to hear the entire conversation. However, the more you find yourself in these sort of situations, the greater the ability to listen with both ears.

Peripheral vision also develops with use, almost as though you possess two pair of eyes as well as two pairs of ears. You may quite often have to deal with groups of people all talking, in which case you automatically exercise more than one sense.

Some people are proficient at listening to two or even three individuals at once as well as employing their peripheral vision to watch and almost hear with their eyes exactly what each person is saying. Those who face this sort of situation daily with their work are usually far more perceptive than others who do not, and quite often possess extremely efficient memories.

There is very little doubt that employing the senses to function outside their normal range of activity causes the precipitation of their development. Perfect retention and recall also develop as a direct consequence.

Study the following four lines of words. See the top word in each line and the one directly below it as a pair. Memorise as many pairs as you can, allowing yourself one minute. When you have done this, change the words around into different suitable pairs and repeat the process.

EGG	ORANGE	TIN	BOTTLE	SAFETY
SHELL	PEEL	CAN	OPENER	CURTAIN

APPLE	*FISH*	*FANCY*	*PICTURE*	*TOP*
PIP	*SHOP*	*FRAME*	*RAIL*	*DOG*

This is an exercise in memory and concentration. Note how long it took you to memorise both combinations of words.

Memorise the words in pairs. See Egg and Shell as one word, Orange and Peel as another, etc. Fixing a long list of individual words in the memory can often be quite difficult, but arranging the words into pairs or even groups makes them easier to memorise.

Installing words in your memory in this way increases your speed and mental capacity. You might like to create your own memory exercise. Make a list of fifty objects, then put them in pairs or groups of three. Take no longer than two minutes to memorise them.

Should you encounter difficulty with a long list of words, instead of trying to plant the whole word in the mind it sometimes helps the process of recall if you focus the attention on the first letter of the word. This procedure is the same as going through the alphabet to remember someone's name. Once you have learned the technique, you should find that the first letter automatically suggests the rest of the word. The memory initiates this of its own accord when it realises what you are endeavouring to achieve.

This method of recollection helps the development of the general awareness and the cultivation of the faculties, thus aiding the general speed of the memory's recalling process.

Persona and Assertiveness

The way you appear to other people is extremely important in the world of business, particularly if you are ambitious and have a strong desire to be successful. The impression you give upon the first meeting is perhaps the most important – regardless of what sort of work you do – as this will be how they see and remember you in the future.

Presenting yourself in a positive, confident way is essential when your job involves meeting a lot of people. If you seem confident, those with whom you come into contact will have confidence in you. Learn to assess situations and individuals simultaneously to enable you to know exactly which approach to take when dealing with them.

Some need to be addressed in a firm, positive way whilst others may require a more sensitive and gentle approach. Personal feelings and mood swings should never be allowed to influence your judgement or attitude towards anyone you meet during the process of your work. Nor should you ever express any signs of displeasure or anger in front of business associates.

Although almost any form of dress is acceptable in the workplace today, a smart appearance is essential. Always be aware of personal hygiene, too, as bodily fragrances are also extremely important when creating a good first impression.

Politeness is a prerequisite when endeavouring to create the correct image, taking care of the way in which you speak. Pay particular attention to diction. Present yourself in all situations with an air of authority without appearing cold, dictatorial or arrogant.

Notice names when they are given to avoid having to say, 'I am so sorry, but your name escapes me.' This does not inspire confidence or give the correct impression.

Work hard at cultivating the correct tone and modulation of your voice. The most effective way is to prepare a couple of sentences on paper and practise speaking into a tape recorder until satisfied that you have achieved the desired tonal sounds.

Making an effort to be meticulous and proficient at work aids the development and cultivation of a good memory. A tidy and well-organised life produces a corresponding effect upon the mind, precipitating perfect and speedy recall.

Understanding your insecurities, faults and failings is a necessity in the development of confidence and the cultivation of character. Believing totally in yourself and what you are capable of achieving is more than halfway to creating a new and more confident persona.

The efficiency of your memory is solely dependent upon how you treat it. Details committed to memory must be carefully filed away, not simply stored untidily. As you become more confident, so your mental agility develops, and the speed of your memory recall increases.

Always make eye contact an integral part of one-to-one conversations. Avoid looking bored or disinterested.

If you need to make a note of the names of those with whom you come into contact do so, at least until you can commit them to memory. Remembering people's names not only gives a good impression but it makes them feel important, too.

14

Visualise Your Way into the Subconscious Mind

One of the most effective methods of releasing the powers of the natural memory is to use visualisation as a means of accessing the subconscious mind. This method of focusing can also be employed to locate something that you desperately need to remember, but for some reason cannot. The process of gaining entry into the innermost recesses of the mind is achieved by presenting before the mental screen specific imagery that will unlock the door leading directly into the memory vaults.

Once the process of visualisation has begun it is important that you follow it through to the end. Make certain that the room in which you are sitting is free of noise and that you will not be disturbed. Any sudden external sound may cause some distress and could also be detrimental to the whole process of the exercise.

The Manor House

Sit quietly for a few moments with your eyes closed. Breathe rhythmically to relax the body and make the mind still. When you feel ready, create a clear mental screen and watch it slowly coming alive.

Imagine you are standing on the steps of an old manor house and that you can see the ornately designed doors slightly ajar. Feel your curiosity drawing you into the house. As you ascend the steps and move towards the doors, watch them slowly open before you of their own accord.

When you enter the shelter of the building, you are overwhelmed with the sense of having been there before. Be reassured by its familiarity and peace.

Follow your curiosity into the main hall directly through the front door. Notice logs roaring in the fire grate. To the left of the fireplace you see a lift. Move towards it. Note how the doors open by themselves.

Step inside the lift and see the doors close. Before it moves, it is important to be perfectly at ease and comfortable.

When you are ready, feel the movement of the lift as it rises. Look at the numerical floor indications moving from zero to one. Notice the lift suddenly stopping.

When the doors open, move from the lift directly onto a long, narrow corridor. On each side, you can see two doors, and at the far end just one door. Select one of them, moving slowly towards it.

Open the door of your choice and move carefully into the room. As you enter, the first detail that catches your eye is a window. By it are a small table and chair. As you move over to the table, you can see a piece of parchment and a pen standing in an ink well.

Take a look around the room. Notice paintings hanging on the walls, an ornate fireplace and a beautiful Persian rug. See logs roaring in the hearth. Hear the sound of crackling wood.

Enjoy the pleasant fragrance in the room. For a moment, feel overwhelmed with a sense of nostalgia.

Spend a few minutes analysing your mood. Change anything that causes discomfort. Alter the room in any way you like. Make certain that you are peaceful and totally at ease during the exercise.

Allow your eyes to move around the room like a video camera scanning its surroundings, noting and recording every detail of the decor and the way in which the furniture is arranged.

Sit by the table. Look upon the piece of parchment as the focal point and filing system for your memory. Know that everything you write on it may be retrieved at any time you enter this room. Once you have mastered the technique of mentally entering the old manor house, you will find it an effective way of recalling anything you desperately need to remember.

To initiate the programme properly, write on the white parchment *Efficient memory, perfect recall*. See this clearly defined. Accept it as a subconscious affirmation. Look at it closely. Read it carefully. Turn the piece of parchment over so that a blank side faces you. Examine it for a few moments, then return the pen to the ink well.

Rise to your feet and look through the window at the beautifully landscaped gardens. Notice the blue sky and the bright sunlight. Make your way slowly over to the door. Taking a last look around the room, move slowly into the corridor.

Make your way along the corridor towards the lift. See the doors slowly open, then enter. No sooner do the doors close when you feel the motion of the lift as it rises. Within moments, it stops moving and the doors open onto the second floor.

Step out of the lift into a round room with a mosaic floor. You notice a high domed ceiling. To the right, there is a large television. As you watch the screen it slowly comes alive.

This will enable you to recall everything from your past. Anything important that you have to remember will be visibly there for you to see on your television screen. All you need to do to initiate the programme is look carefully at your screen and see *Past memories* appear across it. Simply by keying your requirements into the mental television will you be able to access your subconscious mind and retrieve anything you are having difficulty remembering.

You must appreciate that the parchment is for short-term or recent memory retrieval, and the mental television is to remember events from your past. Once you have familiarised yourself with this process of retrieval, you will be able to access your subconscious mind to recall anything. There is no need to activate the television screen on this occasion. Simply be aware of what it is for.

Take one last look at the television screen, then turn and move back into the lift. See the doors close. Feel the lift beginning to descend.

When the doors open, step out of the lift and move across the floor with the fireplace on your left and the logs still burning in the hearth. See the front doors ajar. As they open before you, move from the house and onto the stone steps.

Descend the steps. When you reach the bottom, turn to face the old manor house. Breathe in slowly. As you exhale, allow the picture to fade from your mind.

Upon your entry into the old house you gain access to the subconscious area of the mind. The lift mentally transports the consciousness to the various levels. If there is anything you need to remember, simply take it in to the first level and write it on the parchment. Should you be unable to recall it when required, return to the manor house, for at the first level you will see it clearly written on the parchment.

The television should only be used to access old memories, events that have long since gone from your mind. It may not work immediately. You might have to visit it three or four times. The process is an extremely good way of accessing the innermost recesses of the memory where all our past experience data is stored.

You may need to modify the exercise in some way to suit your specific requirements. I have simply presented this visualisation as an example.

Now that you have concluded the entire programme, you should be well on your way to cultivating a dynamic and efficient memory. Obviously, some of the methods in the programme may not appeal to you. Select the systems that work for you, adapting them as necessary.

The answer to the teaser on page 52 of Chapter Four is nearly always the same – *A grey elephant in Denmark.*

Index